THE KING'S GOLD

THE KING'S GOLD

TRUE WEALTH IS FOUND IN DEEP PLACES

Grace Turner

MONARCH
BOOKS

Oxford, UK & Grand Rapids, Michigan

First published in the UK in 2008 by Monarch Books
(a publishing imprint of Lion Hudson plc),
Wilkinson House, Jordan Hill Road, Oxford OX2 8DR.
Tel: +44 (0)1865 302750 Fax: +44 (0)1865 302757
Email: monarch@lionhudson.com
www.lionhudson.com

ISBN: 978-1-85424-872-5 (UK)
ISBN: 978-0-8254-6277-1 (USA)

Distributed by:
UK: Marston Book Services Ltd, PO Box 269, Abingdon, Oxon OX14 4YN;
USA: Kregel Publications, PO Box 2607, Grand Rapids, Michigan 49501

This book has been printed on paper and board independently certified as having come from sustainable forests.

British Library Cataloguing Data
A catalogue record for this book is available from the British Library.

Printed and bound in Wales by Creative Print & Design.

Dedication

This book is dedicated to Ray Mayhew, whose life of faithfulness and fruitfulness in adversity has challenged and encouraged me to go for true gold for many years.

Acknowledgments

My grateful thanks go to Tony Collins and his colleagues at Lion Hudson who took a chance on an unknown author! Thank you to my husband Nick, to Simon Ponsonby and my friends Janet Drew, Anna Wynn and Sue Grey who, despite my misgivings, encouraged me to write this book.

My deepest love and thanks go to Nick, and to Abi and Dan, my daughter and son-in-law, for their unfailing love and support ... I am so blessed to share my life with you three!

Most of all my thanks go to the One without whom none of this could be written in the first place, who has had patience beyond measure with me all my life, and whose love is the only gold worth mining for.

Contents

	Introduction	11
1	Power or Formula?	15
2	Desert Training Camp	31
3	Stolen Treasure – The Loss of Relationship	55
4	Treasures of Darkness	79
5	Warrior Bride	105
6	The Father is Seeking	131
7	Dividing Your Bread with the Hungry	163
8	The Secret Wealth of Hidden Places	185
9	What is Real?	209
10	A God-Possessed People	223
11	Two Obituaries	239

Introduction

The congregation rose as the organ began to play. They faced the church door and smiled as the radiant bride began to pace slowly up the aisle. Everyone, that is, except the groom. After one long look down the aisle, he whirled back round, put his face in his hands and burst into tears of joy.

That image has stayed with me for some years, as I have thought about the bride of Christ living in what may prove to be her finest and most testing hour. Is she drawing wealth from the King's purse, or is she pursuing 'fool's gold' that may crumble and prove worthless currency in time of war? Is her Groom delighted by the urgency with which she seeks to become his?

The king's purse was simply a name for the royal treasury in the Middle Ages. Individuals were rewarded or sustained from the king's purse, and those of us who are following Christ today know that he has promised to 'supply all [our] need according to His riches in glory…'.[1] Yet increasingly it seems that we encounter seduction by 'fool's gold', counterfeit wealth like goblin gold that disappears overnight. Pyrite is an ore that is named fool's gold because it sparkles, and is gold in colour – but it is brittle and easily cracked, not precious metal.

True wealth is to be found in curious places, and God is preparing and training his bride for battle; he is calling her to seek real gold. So often this is found in pain and tears, in faithful submission during periods in the desert, when with Job we say, 'when He has tried me, I shall come forth as gold'.[2]

The story is told of a beggar waiting for a Maharajah to arrive at his village. He sat all day outside the village hoping to be first to see the Maharajah and ask for alms. When the cavalcade finally arrived, the beggar was indeed ushered into the presence of the great man. He bowed before him and held out his hands, palms up, in traditional gesture of supplication. To his disgust the Maharajah bent forward and did likewise. In great disappointment and frustration the beggar counted out five grains of corn onto the Maharajah's hand and the interview was over. Later as he counted through his grain for his evening meal the beggar saw something glistening. It was a grain of gold! He searched diligently and found five grains of gold, but no more. Suddenly understanding, he cried out, 'If only I had known, I would have given him everything!'

In a culture and a day when everything encourages us to turn inwards in self-gratification, we can lose sight of age-old treasure, or hoard it for ourselves, which is the certain way to lose it. We are going to look at how to pursue true wealth from the King's purse rather than the easily accumulated, flashy but brittle pyrite that leave us cynical, or constantly a prey to new excitement, or to every invitation to re-establish 'meaningful contact' with the King. Old structures *do* need to change with changing times, but they are just that – structures. Gold is obtained the same old way, by mining rich seams in dark places. Isaiah 45:3 says 'I will give you the ... hidden wealth of secret places'.

As we read the scriptures we cannot be ignorant of

the fact that we were born for battle as well as for a crown. In his grace and love for us the Lord is seeking to bring us to a place that is ready, prepared for losses yet assured that the end will see the marriage supper of the Lamb. This is the challenge for us: will we seek instant and insubstantial experiences, or allow God to make us into a fighting unit, a warrior bride? If we do not allow him to do so, we may not be ready when the curtain rises on the confrontation Jesus told us to expect.

Let us embrace the challenge, then, to be those who seek real gold where it may be found, who do not fear testing but see it as the means to prepare for battle and for his glory. Like Queen Esther, the question we face today is, 'If you remain silent at this time, relief and deliverance will arise ... from another place ... [but] who knows whether you have not attained royalty for such a time as this?'

Esther's reply was that she would face the challenge: 'And if I perish, I perish'.[3]

1

Power or Formula?

Gold or Dross?

Have you noticed how desperately we need to feel comfortable? For about six weeks after 11 September 2001, Christians were very serious about their faith and prayer, and many unchurched people flocked to Sunday services and signed up for courses to explore Christianity. After a while everyday life just washed over us once more. The threat was still out there, the serious possibilities hovered on the edge of our consciousness, but the comfort of the familiar took the edge off our prayers and defeated our resolution to seek God in new ways.

Comfort is the enemy of power. Every one of us has to battle with the temptation for our Christian life to become formulaic, because formula are easy. Power comes when the people of God beg and pray and cry for more of Jesus' life to flow through them. It comes when they become so desperate for his resurrection to be worked out in their everyday lives that the society around them cannot help but change. Power is always contested, of course. The battle becomes far more fierce when the gates of hell are under assault from the church of God, but at least the world can see a living God in action through his people!

When I speak to Christians in countries where they are persecuted for their faith, I may hear stories of suffering, pain and hardship, but I rarely hear a word about apathy! Yesterday we were visiting some friends and they said 'Why do we not hear from God through dreams very often? People in other countries seem to hear so much better than we do'. We all decided that busyness and its resultant exhaustion dulled us to his voice, and our emphasis on the material stopped us from being conscious of what is happening in spiritual realms.

In Christian conferences much time is spent discussing ways in which we can appeal to the unchurched, ways of 'doing church better'; and some helpful and creative suggestions have come from them. But the truth is, only the power of God will change the society in which we live, or cut through the devil's lies in those we know and love, and power is the treasure that Jesus bought in blood for his church. Where the power of God is to be seen, there is always a dual reaction in the society around us. Many will be attracted to 'a God who does things', and want to know more. Some will be repelled by the power of God, just as they were when the Son of God walked the earth – people either loved or hated him but they were never indifferent to him!

General Sir Richard Dannatt became Chief of the General Staff in the British Army in August 2006. In the late 1970s he was due to take part in a Remembrance Day parade in Berlin where his regiment was stationed, when he was suddenly struck down and completely paralyzed down one side. The medics thought that he had suffered a stroke, but none of the tests showed any signs of this and they eventually decided that it was a severe cerebral virus. During his time in hospital, unable to move down one side, God spoke clearly to Richard Dannatt saying, that he was only half living for him. His immediate response then and now was to say he would live a full life for his God.[4]

So often we are only half alive! Our missing inheritance is power and instead of this, we seek the fool's gold of entertainment. We are confident that our churches are going well if they are filled with people, and we do not ask where those people are coming from, and why. The church population tends to eddy and swirl in circles, round the great whirlpool of charisma, with an itinerant population chasing the latest 'blessing' or new dynamic preacher or formula. God is saying to us 'Will you only serve me with half your life?' Richard Dannatt was interviewed on *Songs of Praise* a few years ago, and asked to explain why he chose his favourite hymn. His reply was that he had made a vow of allegiance years ago to serve Queen and country, but that he had made a higher and more important vow in his life, and so his choice of hymn was 'O Jesus, I have promised to serve Thee to the end'.

As time passes I realize more and more that starting well is not nearly as effective as finishing well. Being able still to serve God passionately when physical life is frailer and the race goes to the young, praying fervently when ill health confines us to our bed, retaining joy and vision when we are alone suddenly or feel isolated – these are the ingredients of finishing well. Sometimes we start with vigour and enthusiasm, and as time passes, it is not so much the disappointments or difficulties that overtake us, as the fact that we simply become swamped by the cares of this life[5], and lose focus and purpose in terms of our spiritual priorities. Finishing well is recapturing these things, sometimes time and time again, but is never found in leaving the race to the young.

A second generation can come up under great leadership and teaching but unless they win the land for themselves it is just inherited wealth which vanishes like snow. Moses' son did not take over leadership of Israel. Isaac did not have the life Abraham had, and Jacob had to win it back the hard way. The only way for our children to be world-changers is for them to see us gasping for Jesus and his glory, crying out for his power, and moving in the inheritance he bought us; then they will be the same. We need to be in the business of raising another *first generation* that goes on winning land. Somehow with all the enormous emphasis on power, prayer ministry and miracles that we have today, we stand in danger of being second generation. We can spout the buzz words about 'carpet time' and 'being face down', many of us can claim at least one good prophecy over our lives, maybe by someone well known too! So what? We need fresh power, and fresh power is won the same old way every time.

A young missionary asked me how he could move in power. He said he had been reading about some of the great people of God, like Charles Finney who, when filled with the Spirit for the first time, said, 'Wave after wave of liquid love swept over me' – Finney went on to lead revivals all over America. D.L. Moody sought God's Spirit desperately until that wonderful day came: 'O, what a day! – I cannot describe it, I seldom refer to it; it is almost too sacred an experience to name. I can only say that God revealed himself to me, and I had such an experience of his love that I had to ask him to stay his hand'. The young missionary said to me 'How do I get this Grace? I think about it all the time, it is my deepest desire'.

I replied something like this: 'You beg, and cry and hammer on the door. You may get fed up and cynical. You may start believing the hype that everyone else has got it. But you *stay* there begging and crying. A year. Two years. A lifetime if necessary. You say 'I will not let you go until you bless me – *like that* – like Finney and Moody!' Not so that you can write a book about it. Not so that everyone suddenly starts asking you to speak or lead worship. Maybe the very answer to your prayer will take you into heartache and obscurity. But you don't give up until he comes – like that – for you. You don't say, 'Oh well, he came a little bit'. You don't satisfy yourself with busyness. You are scrupulously honest and say 'I'm not going to stop until *that* amount of Holy Spirit anointing comes my way. Even if you have to etch holiness into me with a scalpel. I will not let go until you come, Lord.'

One of the most touching and, as we grow older, sometimes bittersweet experiences that we can have is to see the younger generation blazing with fire for God. We can think, 'I was like that, and I still love the Lord with all my heart, but somehow the flame has died down a bit.' Cynicism whispers, 'When that young person has lived as long as me they won't be flaming like that!' There is truth in the fact that we can't flame up all the time. A fire that is built to last glows deeply within even when there is little to see outwardly. But often, as time goes on, 'we flutter like butterflies around the pole of charisma, or congeal soddenly around the pole of routine'![6]

How are we to live in fresh power, not becoming infantile in our quest for true wealth? Enormously helpful as prayer ministry can be, large numbers seeking prayer will not necessarily mean that the Spirit has come. Every form of service and response can become just another liturgy. In Ross Paterson's book *The Antioch Factor*, the author looks at the church born in Jerusalem, using the account in Acts chapter 2. Surely this must have been the most glorious beginning to any 'ekklesia'? Three thousand converts on the day the church was born, all the major apostles were present, it had everything going for it. Yet by chapter 11, the centre of God's operations seems to have shifted to the church in Antioch. Paterson suggests this is because the Great Commission was to go into all the world, not to stay where we are. It is not that God smites the church which builds its own nest, enjoying its worship and teaching on Sundays – he is a loving Father and blesses us regardless. But we are not fulfilling his commission unless, full of the Spirit's power, we are marching forward into the darkness and taking ground in the lives of those who would otherwise be lost. That is the centre of the Father's heart, and that is where his power is to be found.

'Another Pentecost? Is that what we are waiting for, after the frequent visitations by the Spirit of God in the last one hundred years – Azusa Street, the Welsh Revival, Korea, Toronto, Pensacola, to name but a few? We now have a set of denominations built around and named after Pentecost, as well as the Charismatic move amongst traditional churches, and much, much more. How much more of Heaven's throne gift do we need before we will begin to go? It is true that we need more moves of God – we

need revival urgently, desperately. Yet surely
at the same time we are, by now, on the other
side of "another Pentecost"! We have seen
"an effusion of miraculous gifts, including the
gift of tongues". But what then has changed
with respect to "the commission of Christ as
at first?"[7]

Fresh power, by definition, comes to those who had power
once and need it again. We need to offer back to God our
cynicism and to be realistic, not chastising ourselves for
not being where we once were. We may well have moved
on in Christ, but we need to acknowledge our need for
fresh power. In charismatic circles we can either live the
hype or forget the stories of power, but we need Jesus-life
to be bursting out from the foundation of our being if
our immediate circle of friends and family are to know
his power – to say nothing of the larger world! We need
the true wealth of his power not to gain a reputation but
to pierce the darkness! Do you want to light fresh fires,
and if you do, will you do so whether anyone sees or not?
Mark Buchanan was once speaking at a youth camp, and
he held up two video cases for the teenagers to look at.
One video cover showed Indiana Jones' sweat-soaked
face, surrounded by a Nazi villain, a hooded cobra and a
ship under siege. The other, the cover of a training video,
showed a sewing machine with a piece of cloth and a nice
straight line of stitches! Buchanan asked the teenagers
which cover most captured their view of the Christian life
as evidenced by most churches today. Every one of them
voted for the sewing machine![8]

This is a tragic state of affairs. The blood-bought bride

of Christ, with the eternal Spirit's life coursing through her veins, is living by training manuals and courses! We can all do with learning more, but while we are undertaking just another little bit of training the world goes by on its way to hell, and we find sentences like this extreme. The word for 'anointed one' in Greek is *Christos*. It is Christ! When we are anointed we simply have Christ poured over us and we drip his love, his grace and his power on to those we pass. Every single child of God, no matter how young in the faith, is an heir of his power. Do we spend a few moments each day thinking how it would affect our day if we lived as an heir of all the power of Jesus? Surely it would make a fundamental difference to everything we did.

Wesley said: 'I set myself on fire and men and women came to watch me burn.' How do you set yourself ablaze? Has Wesley's sentence struck you as unusual? He doesn't say 'God set me ablaze', though of course he did. He says 'I set *myself* ablaze'. Fire meant a lot to Wesley. As a child he was rescued from a house fire and his mother called him 'a brand plucked from the burning', something he believed was true both literally and spiritually. One thing I learned during a time of comparatively little blessing in ministry was that you really can set yourself on fire. I do not mean that we are to live in unreality, mouthing platitudes; that surely dries up the spirit. But we set ourselves on fire when we take the obedient choices in secret where no one notices; when we lift Jesus up despite our feelings; when we choose praise over self-pity; when we repeat in faith promises which seem long gone; when we serve others in secret; when we put other people into a place we would like to be ourselves. Real fire means salvation, new vision, fresh hope in the desert, it means standing firm and seeking God … and seeking God … and seeking God … until the fire falls. And the reason it doesn't happen that often is just that it is much easier to follow a formula, or find some undemanding service, than to cry out for any length of time.

When we live in the truth of this, the Spirit sets us ablaze regardless of our temporary happiness or lack of it. Jim Cymbala writes, 'I don't want a title; I don't want to be famous or meet some earthly dignitary; I don't want to be rich. I just want God to clothe me with His Spirit so I can affect people for Christ'[9]. Let's look squarely at what is 'fool's gold' in our lives. Let's look at our protestations of love for our bridegroom and the aching desires of his heart, and let's choose the King's purse. The power he bought us is still available. It will mean tears and prayer, it will mean hanging in there when we are disappointed and lied to by the evil one, it will mean counting the things of this world as worthless 'in view of the surpassing value of knowing Christ Jesus my Lord'[10].

Apparently there was once an argument between John Wesley and Fletcher of Maidenhead. Fletcher said that he would invite those students who wished for more of the Holy Spirit to come into his study and they would shut the door, kneel down and cry for the Spirit to fall upon them, and when he came (like Moody later) they had to 'ask him to stay his hand'. Wesley objected, saying they should never ask him to stop but instead should ask for greater capacity to hold the power he was sending! I wish we had such an expectation of his coming that we could have that argument now!

I remember once asking God that we might leave a legacy after we died. I had in mind some really amazing projects that would rescue people and continue doing so for years to come. I found the Lord whispering that this was not the legacy he wanted us to leave. Not that rescue isn't essential, not that there is no legacy, but that the legacy he wants us to leave is *people* who themselves are first generation lighters of fires, who then give birth to another first generation of men and women who set themselves ablaze for the glorious Lamb. That is the only motive the Holy Spirit takes seriously. He will visit us with as much holiness as we can stand if that is our desire and if we make practical deliberate space for it in our life from this moment on.

Os Guinness once said that on a visit to Australia he met a Japanese CEO who said this to him: 'When I meet a Buddhist monk I meet a holy man in touch with another world. When I meet a Western missionary I meet a manager who is only in touch with the world I know'[11]. I found myself crying out to God as I read that, 'Don't ever let that be us! Lord, let us be holy people who are clearly in touch with another world! Let the dread of God's people fall upon our society as it did when Mordecai and Esther were alive'. Too often we fill people with dread for all the wrong reasons! This was a holy dread, a knowledge that God was with these people, a realization that his power could change the world they lived in.

Pyrite, or fool's gold, is often associated with the presence of gold or copper, and locating fool's gold may mean that the real thing is not far off. This is both encouraging and challenging for the bride of Christ. We can come so close to the source of power but choose the brittle and semi-precious, instead of mining real gold. The semi-precious is to be found in hours of 'soaking' in

God's presence, which do not in their turn lead to change of character and spirit-led action. We have never been so in need of spending time in the presence of the King of kings, but biblical encounter always led to an increase in personal holiness which produced the power of Christ in that person's life. Anything else is pure self-indulgence and will not produce power or life, but introspection which can only stultify. Being in the King's presence means a revelation of his heart, which in turn brings us to real intercession, and intercession, it has been said, is 'the mother of revelation' once more!

Once the longing of God's heart is revealed to us, we still are not ready to move in power. Fool's gold is sometimes also found in a multiplicity of strategies! Sometimes we do clearly see God's heart for the lost and we look at what has worked elsewhere, we go to the conferences, read the books and try to replicate the same results. True power is never imitated. Other people's discoveries can spur us on and envision us, but power is only found by seeking God ourselves, by putting in the hard work and costly time of seeking him until he speaks and moves us. It is found by submitting what we have heard to those who are wise in Christ, and in seeking to implement his instructions at whatever personal cost.

Power is elusive because it does not come when we chase it! There are 'power ministries' just as there are gifts which indicate the power of God: ministries of healing and deliverance. Sadly today these have sometimes become our only definition of the power of Christ, but they are just gifts! Certainly they are gifts which are desperately needed in the Christian church, and they are certainly in evidence when God's power is at work, but the people who move in these things are simply exercising gifts of the Spirit, rather than being spiritual giants! The early church expected such things to happen as a matter of course without any need for stagecraft, but the power we need for daily living is linked with authority. Where you find someone fully submitted to Christ and obedient to him, his authority can be released.

> 'And when Jesus entered Capernaum, a centurion came to Him, imploring Him, and saying, "Lord, my servant is lying paralyzed at home, fearfully tormented." Jesus said to him, "I will come and heal him." But the centurion said, "Lord, I am not worthy for You to come under my roof, but just say the word, and my servant will be healed. For I also am a man under authority, with soldiers under me; and I say to this one, 'Go!' and he goes, and to another, 'Come!' and he comes, and to my slave, 'Do this!' and he does it." Now when Jesus heard this, He marvelled and said to those who were following, "Truly I say to you, I have not found such great faith with anyone in Israel."'[12]

The kind of authority Jesus is speaking about here is not derived from position but from relationship. In John 5 Jesus speaks of doing whatever he finds the Father doing or saying. The key is discovered here by a Gentile centurion. Everything that eminent soldier said was backed up by the might of the Roman Empire. If he said 'Go!' you went! If Jesus told sickness or the demonic to go, it went, because everything he said was backed up by all the authority of

God the Father. Our goal should be to get to the place where everything we do and say is backed up by heaven. The key is to be found in obedience. The Roman soldier was completely obedient to Rome and as a result his authority was defended by a higher power. If we obey the Father, he will allow his power to flow through us into a needy world.

How does this work? Some years ago a friend of mine told me a very amusing story. He had gone shopping in a nearby town, and found himself walking down one of the back streets. Suddenly a piercing alarm went off in a building that he was passing and a man ran along a parapet above him, carrying a bag (of swag, presumably!). He dropped down at my friend's feet, and ran off. My friend chastised himself for not doing anything about it. He was slight in build, not particularly threatening, and extremely unaccustomed to physical violence! In his shame at not acting bravely, he did what all good Englishmen do at such times: he went and had a cup of tea!

While he was drinking his tea he decided what he should have done was to make a citizen's arrest. He walked back to the scene of the crime, to find a crowd had gathered, and the alarm still shrieking overhead. Looking to his right, to his amazement he saw the man who had jumped down in front of him walking past the building looking up at the scene of the crime! Clearing his throat with as much authority as he could muster, he accosted the man and said: 'I saw you run out of there, carrying a bag. You jumped down right in front of me and ran away!' The man (who clearly *was* the offender) grinned cheekily and said 'So what?' My friend cleared his throat again and said 'So I'm making a citizen's arrest!' The man looked at him in astonishment, bent double with laughter, and then strolled off! My friend felt extremely inadequate. After all, if you cannot rugby-tackle the man to the ground, what are you going to do? Of course the whole situation would have been different if he had been wearing the uniform of a police officer. The uniform grants that man authority to act.

Spiritual authority is like an invisible uniform: you either have it or you don't. Jesus spoke 'as one having authority, and not as [the] scribes'[13]. We know godly authority when we hear it. A man or woman who walks with God does not need to tell self-glorifying tales; they speak simply and powerfully with the authority of Jesus. Jesus modelled the flow of power in his life on earth – when the Father said, 'Free that man', Jesus said, 'Come out of him' and the demons fled. When the Father said, 'Heal!', Jesus said, 'Be healed', and the sickness fled. When the Father said, 'Die!' … the Son died. That is where power is won. This speaks of a relationship with the Father of such a calibre, that he can speak and we obey immediately – even to death. This is the power the bride of Christ should be moving in, in our day! We beg for signs and wonders and power and revival but the key is very simple. Are we under authority? Do we come under state authority, the authority of our employer, do we buck the authority in our place of worship? When we are submitted to the Father's authority, and mutually submitted to one another, his power has free access in our lives.

Philip Pullman in his trilogy *His Dark Materials*, calls God 'The Authority'. This is used in a derogatory fashion, intended to show the autocratic rule exerted by God over his creatures. Everything this being does is calculated to end freedom and keep his subjects in submission. Yet our creator's authority is far more like that of a father who stops his child from running into the road, or a watchmaker who gives instructions for the way a clock should be treated if it is to run properly! Can God say no to us and we immediately stop whatever it is? Can he say no to a specific sin in which we may be indulging, or an attitude of self-pity, or criticism, the indulgence of our pet weakness, or even something good which may be the enemy of the best?

I was asked to speak at a wonderful banquet some years back. Many of the guests were ladies from abusive, violent or drug-related backgrounds, who had not been out to something special for a very long time. They were collected by coach, greeted with canapés which would not have disgraced the Dorchester Hotel, given a long-stemmed rose, and escorted to a table laden with delicacies, including a luxury gift in each place. It was thrilling to see their faces as each new treat was revealed, but the thing I found most touching was the reaction of the people putting on the banquet. One after another sidled up to me during the evening and said 'Isn't this brilliant? This is just what God is like, isn't it? Totally lavish in his love!' I found myself thinking that if this is what he's like, then our petty rebellions are just that – petty and immature. We joyfully submit to the loving authority of a lavish Father who is longing to pour out his power on desperate people.

We live in a world where power can be catastrophically misused. We see the evidence daily in our newspapers as we watch politicians, businesspeople, and even church leaders sometimes use their position unjustly. God's power is found when his people take the humble place of prayer in secret; it comes from his Spirit's indwelling presence and their obedience to his whisper. I spoke to someone recently who never enters church but who wanted God to do something about the evil that he was combating through drink and drugs. His friend, who was not a Christian, had told him that God was his only hope! It did not seem incongruous to him to expect God to be able to meet him in power, and he wasn't surprised when he did! It seems to me that sometimes it is only the people of God who do not expect him to do extraordinary things. The world expects it, needs it, longs for it. The Father weeps for his Son's bride to move in her inheritance. Will we move on from the pyrite, which glistens temporarily and gives no lasting satisfaction? Will we pay the price? Will we ask, seek, knock until he pours out Jesus over us and we begin to drip with the abundant life that will change our world?

2

Desert Training Camp

Finding God in Wilderness and Waiting

'Behold, I go forward but He is not there,
And backward, but I cannot perceive Him;
When He acts on the left, I cannot behold Him;
He turns on the right, I cannot see Him.
But He knows the way I take;
When He has tried me, I shall come forth as gold.'[14]

A friend of mine took his Accountancy exams about as many times as it is possible to take them! Finally he passed, and the next thing I heard was that he was lecturing in Accountancy at a local college. Laughingly I said to him, 'How could you possibly be given a job lecturing in a subject you have failed so often?' He replied 'Who better? I have failed from every angle, I am just the right person to teach!'

If that is the benchmark of competence, then I am the right person to write about waiting and deserts! I have found few people who have gone through dry spiritual periods triumphantly, and indeed if one purpose of these times is the trial of our faith, it is likely that we will feel despair and failure during such times.

I often ask people to tell me some words that they associate with a desert. Usually these descriptions include words like 'hot', 'dry', 'boring', 'mirage', 'thirst' and maybe even 'loneliness'. These are all characteristics of spiritual deserts also and the problem with deserts is that they are perfectly biblical. Barren times are not all produced (as the forty years of wilderness in Exodus were) by sin or disobedience. Jesus, *'full* of the Holy Spirit'[15] went into the wilderness and returned *'in the power of the Spirit'*[16]. St John of the Cross terms times like this 'the dark night of the soul', and these words resonate with us because at such a time all the light and joy we once knew in Christ seem an illusion.

There are many causes for a desert or time of spiritual dryness, but we need to know from the outset that ultimately these times train us as men and women who can 'resist in the evil day'[17]. In wartime an invading force will seek to cut off your communications and line of food supply, and a desert may signal that we may be subject to enemy activity or attack. A time comes when somehow we come under a lot of personal pressure in finances, work, home, church, relationships, or all of them at once! There is little time to be nourished by scripture and prayer, we become increasingly beleaguered and isolated and then one day we wake up and communication with God and nourishment by him seem a thing of the past or even of the imagination.

Perhaps arid conditions in our lives can be induced by physical ill health or depression. We can come under condemnation for becoming low, and guilt is piled up either by our own overactive conscience or others' slick evaluation of what we 'ought' to be doing or feeling as a Christian. One of my friends who was suffering from serious depression took the brave step of telling her home group, so that they could support her in prayer. To her dismay she was subjected to a lengthy lecture on her spiritual life and lack of faith! We can and should often be guided by our doctor in these times, and accept the medical help available while still seeking God for his help and outcome. There is no doubt that pain can too lightly be categorized as depression. Nevertheless, when this *is* the cause of a desert time in our life, we should not hesitate to receive the help we can get, without the addition of false guilt or others' perceptions of how long our healing should take.

In my own life I have found that the failure to let go of certain emotions can also hold us in deserts. Bitterness which has not been relinquished can dry up the soul. Without the choice to release someone from judgment we will carry that strain and resentment with us and it can lock out the very saviour we need so much at such times. Pain, which God has begun to heal, but which we do not want to relinquish, can eventually put up a barrier to moving forward in freedom. Military training camps are often situated in desert regions because there are no distractions there, and under these spartan conditions personal weakness is easily detected and dealt with. The end result is a soldier fit for battle, stripped of inessentials, and focused on what really matters. Facing and laying down emotional baggage may take time and pain, but it produces untold wealth in the end.

One cause of deserts can be God himself. In Exodus

23:29–30, God indicates that he allowed Israel to wander in the desert to protect them from a foe that they did not have the strength or maturity to defeat. In Psalm 66:18, the psalmist writes, 'If I regard wickedness in my heart, the Lord will not hear [me]'. Sin that is apparent yet not dealt with will eventually result in spiritual dryness.

A lady working in Christian ministry approached me many years ago to ask if I could arrange a meeting with my pastor for her. There was something in her life that she had never confessed, and it was now making an effective barrier between her and the Lord when she came to pray. On the day of the meeting, I picked her up in my car, and she said to me 'We have a little calendar on the back of the bathroom door where I work, and today's reading was "Deliver us from secret sins"!' The relief of bringing things into the light was overwhelming for her. We need to allow the gentle pressure of God's conviction to alight in our lives. The Lord can sometimes confront us with something, and we shrug it off saying 'I'm sure this is OK, I don't feel any condemnation'. However, if we refuse the gentle persistent conviction of God, things will inevitably dry up in our spirit.

There are times of activity, vision and excitement in our lives, and times of testing and trial, and a vast amount of time in the middle. As we read through scripture we see God's purposes worked out in this middle ground over and over again.

After years of trial and tears, Israel is delivered through the Red Sea and the next chapter is a paean of praise for their salvation. From there they travel straight into a desert with no food or water for three days. In 1 Kings 17, Elijah appears on the scene with a dramatic prophecy followed by a year in the desert. After that he is taken to the widow at Zarephath. This is a crucible, a testing time for Elijah, and two chapters later we find this splendid Old Testament prophet at his lowest ebb. God gives him sleep and sustenance, but when he does speak, it is not with the drama Elijah so loves. God's voice is not always dramatic! Sometimes we feel we are experiencing desert because God never speaks to us in the extraordinary ways that others describe. There is a simple answer to this, and it is praise! As we start to thank and praise God for everything we can think of, perspective returns (this is dealt with in another chapter) but praise also leads to our knowing God's thoughts, because we tell those who love us our secrets. Psalm 103:7 says that God made known his ways to Israel, but his *thoughts* to Moses. Lets not be content with just seeing God's acts but become those who push in to know what he is thinking!

We simply do not know all the reasons why many dry times occur in our lives, but we do have Jesus who has 'been tempted in all things as we are'[18] including deserts, and can walk with us through them. It seems to me that barren times can constitute one of God's most regular and stringent methods of refining gold in us and therefore we should expect treasure to come from these experiences. In Tolkein's *Lord of the Rings,* Aragorn, the coming king, arms himself with a special weapon. It is a sword which once dealt a death-blow to the enemy; in so doing the blade was shattered. The shards of metal were subjected to intense heat and reforged to become a weapon that never leaves his hand. A desert place can become a place of reforging, even in the apparent dark, the heat and the pointlessness that threaten to engulf us at such times.

What, then, are the effects of deserts? We can, it seems, walk through deserts or wander in them. It is an eleven-day walk from the Red Sea to Canaan, and even if you allow for stoppages and large numbers, it shouldn't take 40 years! Heat is a characteristic of deserts and heat is supposed to test us. The apostle Paul says:

> 'Now if any man builds on the foundation with gold, silver, precious stones, wood, hay, straw, each man's work will become evident; for the day will show it because it is to be revealed with fire, and the fire itself will test the quality of each man's work. If any man's work which he has built on it remains, he will receive a reward. If any man's work is burned up, he will suffer loss; but he himself will be saved, yet so as through fire.'[19]

I find that the problem at such times as this is that I feel that if I am being tested by God, I have spectacularly failed the test, so I will have to do it all over again! This is not necessarily the case. Barrenness does not represent a test paper that we will get marked on; it is more like the act of tempering the sword's steel. God is forming us. 'Tribulation [works] patience, and patience, experience, and experience, hope'[20].That is treasure worth having! A soldier that does not learn patience will not live very long to fight another day.

Ken McGreavy says that in the Genesis description of God creating the earth, he was constantly at work, forming and filling. He formed the earth and filled it with vegetation and animal life, he formed the sky and filled it with birds and winged creatures, he formed the sea and filled it with fish. McGreavy goes on to say that God is constantly forming our lives, scooping us out to make more room for being filled with his Spirit. Naturally we all prefer the filling parts to the forming parts! In my case, the seasons of being filled always seem to take much less time, too! I have found it so helpful in understanding God's ways at times of dryness and desert in my life, to see it as a master craftsman scooping out more in order that the container may carry far greater amounts of his glory and hope to thirsty people.

I have a Ming vase at home. These amazing pieces of pottery are beautifully made and then deliberately smashed into tiny pieces before being painstakingly put together to create a far more striking work of art than if the vase had been left. I am familiar with lots of similar illustrations, and usually they fill me with fury when I am the one being 'smashed up'! However, over the many years that the Lord has been at work in me, I have come to recognize the hand of a master in what he brings from these times. The Sahara desert is a place of beauty, even if we may not want to make our home there for long!

One effect of a desert on us is that it helps us to know who we really are. It is very easy to kid ourselves concerning our depth and maturity until beset by a time of dryness or emptiness! Although I may know that God is more interested in my holiness than my achievements, barren landscapes in my life show up just how far I have travelled! I have discovered that at such times I need to react against the right person. If I am under spiritual attack I need to resist the enemy, if I am being formed by God I need to submit, albeit in frustration or tears perhaps. God is quite big enough to take the times when we lash out in pain; we would not have many of the psalms if he were not. However, as we go on in him, we come to trust him even in the darkest valley, because he has trodden the way before us.

There is real strain in keeping up appearances when we are not experiencing God's close presence. One day when I had been preaching and was greeting people at the door afterwards, a lady shook my hand. As she passed, she said, 'You know, it's so hard for me to come to church. Everybody seems so happy all the time and I don't feel I fit in because I am unhappy and struggling right now'. How awful that we cannot be real with the very people we most need to trust, without being loaded with advice or worse, guilt. Sometimes when we have been in groups where people are seeking to be real with one another, we have had this rule: 'No concealing. No condoning. No condemning.' Self-pity has been called the devil's tool to rot away a life. Let us take the painful choices to be real. Let us not let each other hide behind self pity, but let us equally never condemn one another when we are going through pain and trial.

Deserts are boring. The scriptures seem to be dry with nothing to offer and we have the sneaking feeling that they never will again. God kept Israel alive on manna and he kept Elijah alive on morsels. In famine we might dream of three-course meals but the truth is that they would choke us! When last did we give thanks to God for morsels?

It is at such times that we are most susceptible to that most heartbreaking of all desert deceptions – the mirage. A mirage promises refreshment only to disappoint and even mislead us. There are times when we feel we have been doing all right. We are not exactly happy, but have mostly been obedient and walking with God through a dry time. Suddenly everything seems about to change, our hearts lift and we begin to celebrate, only to have another crushing disappointment. It is at these times that we really are in the most danger. We begin to entertain the thought that our faith really is a bitter illusion, and if there is a God he positively enjoys raising us up to deluge us with disappointment again. Satan loves mirages! They form one of his best weapons during a dry time because he knows they can crush us so effectively when our hope is already low.

The enemy also uses mirages in other ways in our lives to lead us into seeking (and often finding) 'fool's gold'. There was a particular time when, as Christian workers, my husband Nick and I lived solely 'by faith' and had the fun of seeing God provide in many creative ways. But a desert time followed hard on the heels of this time of provision. Everything became hard work and lacking in joy, and I found myself daydreaming about what I could do if I won a competition and received a lot of money. I found myself in the grip of rampant materialism even though I (fortunately) couldn't gratify my daydreams! They were a mirage: fool's gold. In surveys, a large percentage of women say they turn first to retail therapy when feeling low, but it is a mirage and will never lead to water.

Charles Revson, the founder of Revlon Cosmetics, said, 'In the factory I produce cosmetics, in the store I sell hope'. Sadly I have known many to slip quietly away from faith in barren times, turning to things that will temporarily fill the void, rather than submitting to the pain of reforging in deep places.

Are there ways to get out of a desert? Of course, if dry times are sin-induced, our repentance will immediately begin to make a way forward, but usually we have to wait it out. Waiting, however, can be passive or active. A friend of mine was praying for me on one occasion when nothing seemed to be happening in my life. She said that a picture of a tennis practice gun came into her mind: 'You will have to wait actively because you never know when the ball will come flying your way!' I realized as she said it that I had always waited passively for God to finally end the boredom.

Isaiah 29:17 says 'In a very short time, will not Lebanon be turned into a fertile field and the fertile field seem like a forest?' (NIV). People can turn a forest to a field overnight, but only God can turn a field into a forest in a short time! He can change the dry barren landscape of our desert very quickly. Joseph was taken from the jail to the second highest position in the land of Egypt and changed his circumstances overnight. We need to wait actively for God, because our enemy is looking to exploit hopelessness at these moments.

Although it may seem cold comfort, it is at these times that we need to keep the spiritual disciplines going. Like Job, we may be in despair but we need to keep talking to God, not to lapse into offended silence which only means we have nowhere left to turn. Equally, even though we may not feel nourished by the word of God at these times, continuing to read it will keep us from falling into despair or falling away from his presence. As we seek ways to genuinely serve Jesus and others rather than drown our own sorrows, perspective returns. Isaiah speaks of choosing to share with those in need, caring for them as we would for ourselves, 'Then your light will break out like the dawn, and your recovery will speedily spring forth.'[21]

I remember when we were personally struggling through a difficult time, that my home group decided they wanted to do evangelism. I felt about as much like doing evangelism as bungee jumping at the time, but I did the things I could do. I cooked the dinner, arranged a speaker and invited my long-suffering neighbours. (These gracious people once came to dinner with us, looked round at the empty room and said 'Where is everyone? No evangelistic activity tonight?') Although I was feeling far from him, I made it possible for God to act and that obedience pushed me forward, giving me hope at a time when I had been marking time in my Christian life.

It is really helpful when we are in that place of dryness to tell God what we are ambitious for. He hears us even if we are not hearing him at the time, and the very act of working out what we want to see in our life in the future gives us space to look at what God can do for us rather than at what he isn't doing for us right now.

Isaiah 35:1–10 spells out – in joyful ringing tones – the promises for those whose experience is the desert:

> *The wilderness and the desert will be glad,*
> *And the Arabah will rejoice and blossom;*
> *Like the crocus*
> *It will blossom profusely*
> *And rejoice with rejoicing and shout of joy*
> *The glory of Lebanon will be given to it,*
> *The majesty of Carmel and Sharon*
> *They will see the glory of the Lord,*

The majesty of our God.
Encourage the exhausted, and strengthen the feeble.
Say to those with anxious heart,
'Take courage, fear not,
Behold, your God will come with vengeance;
The recompense of God will come,
But He will save you.'
Then the eyes of the blind will be opened
And the ears of the deaf will be unstopped.
Then the lame will leap like a deer,
And the tongue of the mute will shout for joy
For waters will break forth in the wilderness
And streams in the Arabah.
The scorched land will become a pool
And the thirsty ground springs of water;
In the haunt of jackals, its resting place,
Grass becomes reeds and rushes.
A highway will be there, a roadway,
And it will be called the Highway of Holiness.
The unclean will not travel on it,
But it will be for him who walks that way,
And fools will not wander on it.
No lion will be there,
Nor will any vicious beast go up on it;
These will not be found there
But the redeemed will walk there,
And the ransomed of the Lord will return
And come with joyful shouting to Zion,
With everlasting joy upon their heads.
They will find gladness and joy,
And sorrow and sighing will flee away.

Campbell Morgan[22] comments on the words in verse 1, 'The wilderness will blossom', saying that in Hebrew the word is literally 'to spin'. He says 'That is more than poetry, it is science. Every movement of life is a spinning, whirling movement.' When we are spinning we lose all sense of direction. The fact that we are in darkness certainly does not mean God is inactive. Genesis 1 assures us that when everything was formless and void the Spirit of God was hovering over the chaos, creating life.

But there is truth, too, in the fact that 'the wilderness will (literally) blossom'. Scientists have raised polydomes in the desert which extract moisture where you would imagine no moisture existed, and seedlings suddenly appear. The promise is that the very things that are hurting us at this moment will be the ones to grow and yield fruit later, just as the irritants in an oyster create a pearl.

Isaiah continues to say that the yield will be profuse and that which has no strength will be reinvigorated (Isaiah 35:2–3). Lack of hope can sap our physical and emotional strength and resources, but when the time of renewal comes we will 'gain new strength' (Isaiah 40:31). 'He will save you' (35:4). The name of Jesus is written all over the Old Testament. Every time we see the word salvation it is the Hebrew word 'Yeshua', so the promise of salvation here is a promise of Jesus himself coming to end the desert time. After that vision will be restored and we will hear his voice again. What a wonderful hope when all seems dark and silent.

Our tongue will be free to praise again and the mirage will become a pool. No more false hopes, no more insubstantial fool's gold; true hope and substance are coming! The chapter ends by speaking of the road to which all this wandering has in fact been leading us. A highway of holiness may be uncompromising, but it is such a relief when we have been wandering in confusion! We are protected from the enemy by fellowship with the redeemed (often we have cut ourselves off from this just when we need it most) and the joy returns.

In her beautiful book *Hind's Feet on High Places*[23], Hannah Hurnard tells the allegory of a child called Much-Afraid who has a crooked mouth and a limp, and desperately wants to love and be loved in return. She trusts in the Shepherd to lead her to the 'high places' and eagerly looks forward to meeting her guides for the journey – imagine her horror when she discovers their names are Sorrow and Suffering! However, after much wandering and trial of her faith, when the final transformation comes, Much-Afraid is given a new name: Grace-and-Glory, and she discovers that her companions, Sorrow and Suffering, have likewise been transformed into Joy and Peace. The King's purse is full of treasure. In deserts we cannot imagine anything that could possibly be worth all the pain and emptiness, yet what is worked into our lives will be beyond price.

Longing and waiting is part of living in a fallen world. 'For we know that the whole creation groans and suffers the pains of childbirth together until now. And not only this but we ourselves groan within ourselves, waiting eagerly for our adoption as sons, the redemption of our body.'[24]

When my daughter was five years old, a student we had known well asked me privately if Abi could be her bridesmaid the following year. As a teacher the bride-to-be knew that you should never tell a small child about an exciting event too early. Unfortunately I was not quite so discerning! I told her about the coming treat one day when she needed some cheering up, and for the next nine months she perpetually wanted to know when we would be starting for the church. The final weeks were agony for all of us! The whole episode reminded me forcibly of Jesus' words that we should be like bridesmaids, waiting on tiptoe as it were for the bridegroom's appearing: 'Is it now, Lord?'

When Jesus was baptised by John, the Holy Spirit descended on him like a dove, and he went straight into the wilderness. Simeon spent much of his life waiting for something he had been promised. Eugene Peterson[25] says that at times like this we are (like Simeon) to be like watchmen. Watchmen do not change the world, they don't appear to do anything much, but it is their duty to stay alert to danger and to watch for the dawn.

We have our eye on the future, on God blessing us, making us famous, or married, or wealthy or happy – or all of them! God has his eye on us. In waiting times I am usually thinking, 'When I get out of this time I can get to do this or that', but actually God is forming my character now, in the waiting. The eleventh-century monk, Brother Lawrence, wrote the much-loved little classic *The Practice of the Presence of God*[26]. His work duty comprised presiding over the monks' kitchens yet over the washing up and preparation he was able to practice being in the presence of his Lord.

The Africans have a saying: 'The Swiss may make the watches, but we Africans – we have the time!' (If you have ever lived in Africa you know exactly what they mean!). It seems that we in the West spend the first half of our life waiting for something to happen: 'When I'm a teenager', 'When I'm 21', 'When I'm married', 'When I get that promotion', 'When that person leaves'… Then as we get old we spend significant amounts of time looking back. I love the Peanuts cartoon where Lucy takes the psychiatrist's chair and intones, 'Charlie Brown, people are like travellers on an ocean liner. Some of them have their deckchairs facing the front and eagerly look into what the future has for them. Some of them have their deckchairs facing astern and are always looking back. Which are you, Charlie Brown?' Charlie Brown ponders for a moment and then says, 'I can never get my deckchair to open'!

How are we, the Easter people who have resurrection life within us, meant to live in the waiting times? Whether we are waiting for a promise to be fulfilled or when we just feel we are marking time in the humdrum of life, there are ways of waiting actively. There are some answers for us in Luke 24 where Jesus gives final instructions to his disciples before his ascension. They are about to enter a time of waiting before his power is unleashed through them.

First of all, Jesus tells them to *stay in the city*[27]. He is saying in effect 'Don't run off looking for my power to come here, there or somewhere else. Just stay where you are and look for my deliverance.' Many of us live our lives like ministry junkies, waiting for our next shot in the arm from a conference or someone designated to hear from God for us. We need ministry when we are at low points and we need someone else to listen to God for us or just to pray for us. However, there are many times when God is at work changing us in the silence, he is hovering over the chaos[28], and no amount of asking others for help will move us on until he has worked his image into us like pressing a signet ring into soft wax.[29]

Millions have been spent on chasing about the world to get a fresh touch from the Lord, but there is an old hymn that puts it this way:

> *My goal is God himself,*
> *Not joy or peace*
> *Or even blessing*
> *But himself*
> *My God*[30]

It is when nothing is happening and we hang on in faith and tears, sometimes in frustration, self pity and faithlessness, but we still hang on, these very times are the ones where he is forming his image in us.

One of my favourite episodes in the life of Joseph can be found in Genesis 40:8. God has given Joseph dramatic dreams of greatness, followed by betrayal, slavery and eventual imprisonment. His fellow prisoners, the butler and the baker, both receive dreams one night and go to Joseph for interpretation. What would you or I be tempted to say at such a moment? 'Dreams, huh? You certainly don't want to listen to them! They are mirages and get you into nothing but trouble!' Not Joseph! He replies simply, 'Do not interpretations belong to God?' The once-cocky lad with dreams of grandeur has been reforged through tribulation and waiting into a man of faith.

Lawrence of Arabia wrote these memorable lines: 'Some men dream by night in the dusty recesses of their minds and wake to find their dreams have vanished. But those dreamers of the day are dangerous men. For they may act upon their dreams and make them happen.'[31] Have your dreams evaporated? Are you feeling disillusioned and cynical? I am reminded at such times of Aslan's words to Lucy in C.S. Lewis's *The Last Battle*. Lucy begs Aslan to help the dwarves to see the reality of his provision rather than the chaos and mess that they are experiencing. Aslan says to her, 'Their prison is only in their own minds, yet they are in that prison and so afraid of being taken in that they cannot be taken out'[32]. Cynicism brings us to that place – all of us experience it from time to time. The brave are those who choose to risk once more.

During a waiting time, it is usually right to stay where God has put us, even though that seems the hardest place on earth. Our mind darts in all directions looking for ways of escape, the grass always seems greener elsewhere and we are tempted to lose vision or doubt that it was ever real. This is the time to stay where we are. In the army you obey the last order of the commanding officer until another is given. This is a time for restating the promises he has given us, even when they seem to mock us; to speak them out again rather than abandon them or wrap them in tissue paper to be occasionally looked at with regret. Active waiting is hard because we are keyed up. Waiting for a practice gun is a picture of tension, of focus, and it is tiring. How do we remain focused if, like Joseph, we have had years of waiting? Fool's gold seems altogether more attractive at such times: something – anything – to distract us and take us away from the reality of the present. Dangerous options suddenly begin to beckon – a sudden change of scene or employment, an illicit relationship, anything to distract us from the everyday tedium of the desert place.

So firstly Jesus told the disciples to stay in the city after he was no longer physically with them. They needed to stay focused; they had watched him ascend and they needed simply to return to Jerusalem to wait for his next move. They could have rushed off shouting his resurrection to all who would hear it, pre-empting the power released at Pentecost, but the challenge he left them with was to wait. So often when God begins to reveal something to me, I am so delighted that I rush off to tell someone. I am slowly realizing that if I will wait, he will often pull back the curtain on far more that he has to say to me. I felt some time ago that the Lord spoke very simply to me, saying, 'You want too much history and too little mystery'. In other words, too often I want to turn my deckchair towards the stern of the boat and look back at what I know, at what is safe, when God is waiting to show me 'the mystery of godliness'³³. The disciples needed to wait because they were waiting for the power to change the world!

There is age-old wisdom to be found in Solomon's injunction 'Whatever your hand finds to do, *do it with all your might*' (Ecclesiastes 9:10, italics mine). If we are in secular employment we can ask God for one person to intercede for. We can ask him how we can be like Jesus in that place today, and see what creative plan he comes up with. We can rebuild our time with him or give something up in order to do so. Because waiting and desert are dangerous times, giving up the one friendship that seems hardest (our friendship with him) is the quickest way to despair. While we are not meant to spend these times in hand-wringing condemnation, we do need to check that nothing in our own lives is hindering God from moving. Stephen Hill writes 'God doesn't want acts of contrition from us, he desires a lifestyle of obedience.'³⁴

There are other things we can do to focus and wait actively. One challenge I have found helpful is to pray for someone else to be more blessed than we are! I remember once being challenged to this sort of unselfish praying (something the Lord delights to answer), so my husband and I decided on a couple to pray for, and I suddenly received a rude awakening – I didn't want them to be more blessed than me! I had been waiting so long for God to act in my life, I felt positively outraged that he might move in their lives first! Our commitment to pray in this way released something ugly and self-centred inside me, and helped me to trust that he who wanted to do my friends good loved me just as much: another little nugget of gold slipped from the King's purse into the shrivelled place in my heart at that moment.

As we wait it is a good time to remind God with thanksgiving of his promises to us, telling him that we love him for *himself*, not for his promises, and that we trust him because he cannot lie. One morning, during a particularly dry time, I woke to find my small daughter at my bedside. 'Mummy, which book in the Bible looks like a calculator?' she said. I sat up in bed groggily and tried to focus. 'God gave me a picture for you. It's a calculator with 2319 on it' she explained. Together we looked at the contents page of my Bible and got to the book of Numbers! As we looked up Numbers 23:19, God's word leapt out of the page at me: 'God is not a man, that He should lie, Nor a son of man that He should repent; Has He said, and will He not do it? Or has He spoken, and will He not make it good?' It is remarkable how our affirmation of truth lifts a heavy spirit! The enemy's first temptation to the woman in the garden hisses in our ear at such times, 'Has God said...?'

As we affirm his word, our faith begins to rest not in the future, but in the one who holds and moulds that future for his divine purposes.

As those first disciples waited in Jerusalem, they spent their days in worship and prayer[35]. You would think at empty times in our lives it would be easier to spend time focusing on Jesus but despair can make it all but impossible. A choice to worship frees the heart once more – it is actually the very best way to stay focused. It is not the tension of the tennis court, it is the action of the lover constantly turning his thoughts to the one he loves. A friend of my father's placed a photo of his loved one on his watch so that he looked at her face each time he needed to tell the time. Personally I cannot think of anything more irritating! I prefer the story of the Salvation Army officer who had the words engraved on his watch 'Every hour for Jesus'.

I do not know how I would have got through some of the waiting times without worship, as nothing unlocks the wealth of the King's treasury more effectively to us. We will look at this further in another chapter. When I look at God's loving kindness and patience, at his faithfulness and grace, the fact that I am waiting assumes a right perspective. If I focus on the circumstances I can become bitter, disappointed or lethargic, but it is possible to look beyond them and speak to the one who will act in love once again in my life, and who in his grace is shaping me for his purpose.

Wang Ming Dao, the wonderful Chinese Christian who was imprisoned for over twenty years, was interviewed by a Western Christian on his release from prison. When asked what it had been like the great old saint replied in the words of an old English hymn:

'All the way my Saviour leads me
What have I to ask beside?
Can I doubt His tender mercy
Who through life has been my guide?
Heavenly peace! Divinest comfort!
Here by faith in Him I dwell
Since I know whate'er befall me
Jesus doeth all things well'.[36]

Fanny Crosby, who wrote those lines, was blind; she needed one to lead her who knew the way and she, like Wang Ming Dao, did not doubt his 'tender mercy'. I am told that in the days of using the bow and arrow for warfare, an archer would have one special, 'select' arrow that he would keep for the most important occasion. You can imagine him getting out that arrow and sharpening it from time to time, but if the arrow was not inanimate you could imagine it thinking, 'He isn't using me for what I am made for!' But the day will come when that arrow will be used to fly to its goal and bring down the target. Isaiah 49:2 says, '…in the shadow of His hand He has concealed Me; and He has made Me a select arrow'. Emerson said, 'A hero is no braver than an ordinary man but he is brave five minutes longer'. A hero surely waits out deserts five minutes longer also!

When hardship or pain come to us we can respond like Joseph, or as his father Jacob did. Jacob appeared to give up after he heard of Joseph's death. He lived in terror that another of his sons would be taken from him. Fear and hurt appeared to paralyse his ability to hear from God for years. Joseph has resurrection life in the worst of circumstances, and he goes on hearing from God even when everyone else has forgotten his existence!

The Egyptians gave Joseph a new name, Zaphenath Peneah. It means 'The Lord speaks – he lives'! A man who had been promised much and watched it all slip through his fingers, a man who has been deeply betrayed and who must have often been disillusioned, is given an amazing, faith-filled name. His life, faithful as it has been in the years that are not recorded for us, has become a visible boast to those looking on, that God speaks, he lives!

Joseph's first son is named Manasseh: 'made to forget'. Wang Ming Dao knew something of that grace from God. Joseph is made to forget the pain by the near presence of his God and the fulfilment of age old dreams. The long and painful labour is over and the new birth eclipses all that went before it. '"Shall I bring to the point of birth and not give delivery?" says the Lord.'[37]

But it is the second son, the son who transcends Manasseh in importance, whose name is beloved of all who wait. His name is Ephraim, 'Fruitful', for Joseph said 'God has made me fruitful in the land of my affliction'[38]. Not fruitful because of affliction, not fruitful since affliction but fruitful in that hard place.

We need to ask God in his grace to save us from running after fool's gold at these times. As Eugene Peterson says:

'We try to get [joy] through entertainment. We pay someone to make jokes, tell stories, perform dramatic actions, sing songs. We buy the vitality of another's imagination to divert and enliven our own poor lives. The enormous entertainment industry in our country is a sign of the depletion of joy in our culture. Society is bored, a gluttonous king employing a court jester to divert it after an overindulgent meal… But there is something we can do. We can decide to live in response to the abundance of God, and not under the dictatorship of our own poor needs. We can decide to live in the environment of a living God and not our own dying selves. We can decide to centre ourselves in the God who generously gives and not in our own egos which greedily grab.'[39]

This is the wealth that we so often fail to grasp: the face of Jesus is etched into us during times of waiting, falling, and choosing to rise again. Disappointment often blurs our eyes with tears and makes each day seem long, wearying, pointless. However, if we do not run after fool's gold at this time to ease the pain, then wealth is to be found in hidden places of the heart. We find that the storehouse of our spirit that we thought was bare has grain enough to feed us on our journey.

3

Stolen Treasure – The Loss of Relationship

The Price of Praying

'Anthony Bloom tells the story of an elderly woman who had been working at prayer with all her might but without ever sensing God's presence. Wisely the archbishop encouraged the old woman to go to her room each day and "for fifteen minutes knit before the face of God, but I forbid you to say one word of prayer. You must just knit and enjoy the peace of the room".

The woman received this counsel and at first her only thought was, "Oh how nice. I have fifteen minutes in which I can do nothing without feeling guilty!" In time however she began to enter the silence created by her own knitting. Soon she said "I perceived that this silence was not simply the absence of noise, but that the silence had substance. It was not the absence of something but the presence of something." As she continued her daily knitting she discovered that "at the heart of the silence there was he who is all stillness, all peace, all poise". She had let go of her tight-fisted efforts to enter God's presence and, by doing so, discovered God's presence already there.'[40]

I heard a story recently about a young Christian drama student who was confronted with an unusual drama exercise. The tutor asked the students to gather in a circle while he blindfolded someone in the centre. The students were told to think loving and positive thoughts about this guy, and the blindfolded young man had to walk forward and stop in front of the person he felt the most 'positive energy' from! He stopped in front of the Christian student.

The tutor asked what positive thoughts she had been thinking and she replied that as she had not known quite how to do the exercise, as she was a Christian she had decided to pray for the guy. A little put out, the tutor said, 'OK, let's do it again'. Everyone moved round, and the blindfolded student made his way to the same girl! Mildly freaked out, by this time, the tutor said 'Let's do it one more time' and the same thing happened! At this point the tutor commanded her not to pray next time! She agreed, and to everyone's relief the blindfolded student stopped in front of someone else. The tutor turned to this new student and asked him what *he* had felt towards the man in the centre. He replied, 'Well I saw that praying seemed to work for her, so I thought I'd give it a go!'

Perhaps the greatest single inducement to make God's people seek fool's gold rather than his abundant, outpoured treasure, is the enemy's chief source of delight

– a lack of real comprehension of true encounter with God, and the wealth of relationship that would follow if we sought it. Our enemy (and his) is so clever at distracting us from this, the most valuable of all priorities in our lives. He is adept at loading us with guilt and condemnation on the one hand for not making time for prayer, and a misplaced caution against legalism on the other, saying that we are loved whether we meet with him or not so we must not get into a mindset of 'duty' that will kill relationship. Of course there is truth in this argument but either way we simply miss the fact that he is stealing the one true treasure.

The enemy lost this gold many years ago, the treasure of relationship, of time spent in the presence of truth, beauty, mercy, fatherhood – time that transforms us more truly than any of the other areas we will touch on in this book put together. When we speak of 'stolen treasure' we usually mean that a malign person takes something belonging to us and it becomes their property. This is not so with the treasure of relationship. The enemy, Satan, is subtle in his strategies, and his gain is not the relationship we lost, but the pain of the Father spurned. He takes care, sometimes, not so much to touch our devotional times, merely to snatch our encounter with the Father. Structure can drown out encounter as effectively as busyness or our choice for silence.

Many helpful books have been written on the subject of prayer, yet encounter with our father on a daily, hourly basis, is still a struggle and will continue to be so for the bride at war. Nevertheless, if we do not find that place, we will effectively be robbed of reality in our faith, and the Father will be robbed of our sonship, the purpose for which he created us. We sit in a combined conspiracy at Sunday services and fellowship groups, most of us assuming that the others are having a better time at encounter than we are, and because we do believe in God and love him, we continue to play the Christian game with varying success. Those of us who are Christian workers can be best at this little charade, I know – I have played it all too often. We work for him, we search the scriptures, we speak in faith, but we can remain robbed of encounter.

Many years ago, my family visited England from South Africa. We did not realize that in two short years we would be coming back to live here and so, being good colonials, we sought to steep ourselves in what we perceived to be the British way of life! My mother was particularly keen on shepherds and sheepdog trials…I remember freezing on many occasions while she watched, fascinated, as the little dogs modelled immense dexterity and obedience in herding their flocks. One day we were driving through Scotland and to my mother's delight we saw a shepherd and his sheep in the sloping field to the left of us. The shepherd was at the top of the field and the sheep down near the noisy, busy road. The little sheepdog was running backwards and forwards but it was clear that he could not hear the shepherd's whistle. Finally the sheepdog left the sheep, raced up the field and sat at the shepherd's feet, listening to instructions after which he returned and rounded up the flock perfectly! My mother often reminded me of that story as I grew up, and the fact that it was more helpful to encounter the shepherd than race about trying to do his work.

Jeremiah lived in the priests' town of Anathoth. The two names of the prophet and his home town are important to us if we want to reclaim the treasure that is ours in Christ. Jeremiah means 'God will rise' and Anathoth means 'answers (to prayer)'. Jeremiah is one of the many Old Testament prophets who suffered deeply for their faith, and he comes at one of the darkest moments of the nation's history. His name is a cry of hope in the darkness – 'God will rise!' – and he lives in a place called 'Answers'. I want to live in the place of answered prayer, not because it is a place of miracles (though there will be some along the way) but because it is a place of encounter. God does not answer in the way man answers, he does not answer in the way I want him to answer. Sometimes he is silent for far longer than I consider right or fair! But his presence is the place I want to live in and cultivate more than any other and it will, in the end, bring the answers I need to live by.

It may seem obvious but when we pray we need to get right in to God's presence. Evangelicals can be a bit presumptuous. We say (and it is true) 'God is everywhere. He knows my every thought, I am never out of his presence'[41]. We say (and it is true) 'God loves me, I don't need a specific time in prayer, I can talk to him as I walk along during the day'. However, I am firmly convinced that my lack of power and authority as a Christian, my lack of seeing the living God in action is often simply because of lack of encounter. Our marriage relationships, our relationships with our children or our friends will founder when we do not spend quality time with those whom we love – our heavenly Father is no exception. One young man told me his relationship with God was similar to his relationship with his doctor, 'I only go when I have to, and I am embarrassed at wasting his time!'

Some years ago I visited Romania and was praying with a vivacious young student at the Bible School. She told me that although she was outwardly cheerful, she felt deeply rejected. Her father had, according to her mother, tried to kill her when she was a baby, and her mother left him because of it. Her stepfather had abused her, and she could see no way that she could relate to God as a father. I reminded her of Jesus' words to Philip: 'He who has seen Me has seen the Father'[42] and we prayed that Jesus would show her the Father. After a moment she said, 'Well actually, I can't imagine Jesus, either!' Rather desperate, I went further back and said 'The Holy Spirit makes Jesus real to us, so let's ask him to start there and do that for you.' After praying together for a while, she said that Jesus' compassion and care for her had become a reality to her heart for the first time. So I said 'Lord Jesus, would you make the Father real to his daughter now'. I will never forget what happened next. Slowly – infinitely slowly – the girl's hand stretched out (her eyes were closed) and as my friend and I watched suddenly both her arms tightly clasped her chest as though she was hugging someone and the tears poured down her face. She slowly opened her eyes and said, 'As we were sitting there, I felt Jesus take my hand and then I saw the most enormous figure you could possibly imagine! I ran into his arms and he hugged me so tightly!'

One might say, 'Well maybe that girl needed an encounter like that. I am not visual in that way and God does not speak to me like that.' Scripture is full of the multitude of ways he speaks – through his word, through the Holy Spirit's nudges as we are living our life, through the gifts of the Spirit or in ordinary circumstances. The important thing to realize is that the Father wants to encounter his children. We reduce prayer to formula because formulas are so much easier to retain than relationships! Relationships take time and effort. They can grow cold. They demand our involvement and so gradually the enemy entices us with fool's gold instead of the treasure we were meant to enjoy every day, every moment of our life.

Of course if we do not know him, we cannot function in the way we were made for. If man is made to 'run on God' the way a car runs on petrol, then not knowing God will be crucial to us. Every demand that God makes of us in the scripture relies on the fact that we were made to be filled with God! Without that ingredient every demand is not only unreasonable, it is completely impossible!

When Buckingham Palace first opened to the public, my husband and I took our daughter and her friend to see inside the hitherto private domicile of the Queen of England. I remember entering one long high-ceilinged, sparsely-furnished chamber which was clearly furnished to inspire awe. There was a long red carpet leading to a dais, on which sat two incredibly large thrones; everything in this room inspired feelings of remoteness and inequality. I found myself thinking about the young princes at the time, and the fact that they would probably not experience either of these emotions when they entered that room, because for them love was always on the throne, making it home for them. Prayer is fundamentally finding a way to come to that place, the place of encounter, where we approach an awesome throne on which love is seated, making it our home. Our experience of fathering may have been good, bad, or remote, but Moses affirms, 'the Lord your God carried you, just as a man carries his son'.[43] A loving father often carries his son high on his shoulders – a position of pride and a position of safety. Many creative friends of mine have shared with me their solutions for carving out space to encounter their Father. One young man who was a teacher found that he could not get up any earlier to pray and that when he finally got home, life had a way of taking over. His solution was to stop the car on the way home. In the winter he would stop in a petrol station and get some coffee, and then sit in the car and spend time encountering his Father. People with complicated lifestyles can still find ingenious solutions for seeking the King's purse and the gold of his presence.

One of my good friends said that when he became a Christian he regarded prayer rather like an exercise machine. He would 'assume the position' and effectively fight against the weights until he had accomplished what he felt he should do for the day! One day he realized that there was a relationship to be revelled in, and that his Father wanted to talk to him as much as he wanted to do the speaking! Letting him in to every corner of the heart can be grim, but it is the crucible that will melt and remake us. We hide in people and in Christian advice – but God himself wants to communicate at the deepest level with his children

For me prayer is hard because I am so achievement orientated and it can feel like dead time! One day I decided that I would seek God in prayer earlier than usual. I confess to feeling somewhat smug when I came to the place of prayer, and when I sensed the Lord asking me the question 'Why are you here?' I knew the answer! 'Because prayer is the place of power,' I replied glibly. There was a pause and I felt the Lord simply challenge me with the words 'I had hoped you just wanted to be with *me*'. I moved swiftly on with what I felt sure was a winner and asked him to show me his heart. To my surprise the answer was 'No'. Suddenly I realized that we do not just spill out our deepest secrets to someone who has never spent quality time with us, so I said 'Lord I will spend time with you, and if you do not want to speak to me that is fine, but I want to hear you more than I want to speak to you.' For a number of days things were pretty quiet! I had a strong sense that the Lord did want to speak to me, though, and that if that was the case, I wanted to hear it and was prepared to wait. One day I had a clear picture in my mind's eye of someone pulling back the covering over their chest to reveal a large gaping hole surrounded by bruises. It was obvious that to move would be excruciatingly painful.

I asked the Lord about it and he said it was a picture of how he felt. Smaller individual bruises represented people – a child who had been abused, or brutally assaulted, a person who had grown up bitter and twisted, out of his plan; someone like myself who did not care sufficiently for people like this. The bruises scaled up to large, corporate sins and injustices. I sensed the Lord was telling me he wanted to speak to me about these things daily, so for the next five months I came before him and asked him to speak to me about the things that were breaking his heart. The thing I found most worrying was my own lack of emotion. I observed the things that were breaking his heart, I even prayed about them, but there were no tears. I realized that this was the state of God's people, seeing daily pain and misery but somehow inoculated against any emotion or anguish.

One day everything changed. I was praying as usual, that morning, when again the Lord gave me a visual illustration. I saw a figure bent over double, groaning and groaning and groaning. I knew somehow that this was Jesus and as I watched he showed me a river, full of people who appeared to be twisted and reduced. He said, 'This is the number of people who, even as we speak, are going into a Christless eternity, and this is what breaks my heart'. I began to realize that we are not meant to be preaching necessarily to the unconverted about hell. We *must* speak to them of the love and mercy of Christ, but it is essentially the church, his blood-bought bride, that needs to know about hell. Jesus was the one who spoke about hell the most, because it broke his heart! I realized in that moment that even if I had had pain and suffering every day for my whole allotted time on earth (and some people do have that), that eternity would more than eclipse that pain. But hell is the worst possible agony we can imagine, both magnified and perpetual. This is why the Lord, our loving Father, calls us to encounter... for our sakes, but also for his sake! To hear his heart and to know his will. We will never be the same when that happens.

They say that the chief enemy of love is a distracted gaze. We see young lovers gazing into each other's eyes and we are tinged with sadness when after a while that stops. 'Revival comes when people get dissatisfied with what is and yearn deeply for what could be.'[44] God is calling his people today to go beyond the place they have come to in the Spirit and to enter deeper into his presence and holiness if they want him to come to them like that in this day. People pray 'More, Lord, more!' over one another but the question we have to ask ourselves is why we want more. Is it for our own satisfaction, or is it for his?

When asked how much money was enough to satisfy, John Paul Getty famously said, 'Just a little more'. I thought about this when I was visiting a friend who was serving God in another country. I was saying how happy he must be to see the number of people who were coming to Christ and he replied, 'For me it is never enough. I remember when I led over sixty people to Christ one week, and I was left still with profound dissatisfaction that more had not come to him'. I thought of John Paul Getty's 'just a little more' and thought that phrase showed where our true wealth lies. Where does our heart yearn for 'just a little more' – that is where our heart's true passion lies.

J.H. Jowett tells the story of Bishop Burnett, years ago, riding through the crowd when an old lady accosted him. Lifting up a crust of bread and waving it before him she cried out, 'All this! All this – and Christ!'[45] If our first passion, our true wealth, is the presence of God then that is what we will be crying out and seeking for today. We will never live and move in the way Jesus did on this earth by increased knowledge, only by *increased access*.

The writer to the Hebrews tells us:

'But you have come to Mount Zion and to the city of the living God, the heavenly Jerusalem, and to myriads of angels, to the general assembly and church of the firstborn who are enrolled in heaven, and to God, the Judge of all, and to the spirits of the righteous made perfect, and to Jesus, the mediator of a new covenant, and to the sprinkled blood, which speaks better than the blood of Abel.'[46]

In our day we have learned that there is so much more to be had from God, and we cry out to him in worship and he comes to 'our place'. That is what happens when we have a ministry time so often – he comes to us, in our time frame (whether a Sunday service, in our private prayer time, or at a conference etc.,) and we receive more of him. Entering is the next step… *we* go to *his* place! Hebrews 12, referring back to Mount Sinai, reassures us that we have not come to blazing fire, darkness, gloom and whirlwind, even though these things are an expression of God's character. We have come to a place where, against all the odds, we belong.

If we read Revelation chapter 4, we see the awesome immensity of the power we approach when we come to pray. We come to a place. A place that one day is going to be home, so we might as well make it home now. The city of God, the place where God and his angels and those who have died in the faith are all dwelling right now, is not 'above the bright blue sky' as the old children's hymn has it, but simply another dimension going on right beside us. We need to find this place in prayer and stop making excuses. We are in a serious day and the Lord is calling his people to know him deeply so that they may have power to shake the world. If we stay in our place, the place of need and being serviced by his dear Holy Spirit, he will allow that. When I was first a Christian I was told 'You can have as much of the Holy Spirit as you want'. I am starting to understand that now. If we only want a little bit of his presence, that is what we will receive. But I believe God is beginning to call the church and individuals to recognize that the deeper we go, the wider will be our sphere of ministry. Wherever God has descended, over the centuries, with the weight of his glory, you will always find there have been people 'praying the price' and today he is calling his bride to stop mouthing platitudes of worship and to take her position as the intercessor he most wants to hear.

When we enter his presence, we have come to a people. Hebrews 12 begins by reminding us of them... all who have gone before us like a huge heavenly Olympic stadium crowd, watching as we run, cheering us on, knowing all the temptations and tiredness we face and shouting to us to go for gold, not to settle for applause. We have come to a judge – this isn't something we like to emphasize often today. We love the Father-heart of God, and rightly so, but Jesus talked a lot about our coming before a judge. We simply will not receive power today without holiness, or if we do it is either short-lived or dangerous, because we have not built that cast iron mercy seat for the power of God's holy presence to sit on.

We have come to Jesus and his sprinkled blood. Do we take time consciously to come into his presence when we come to pray? I have to confess that so very often I just come to get my prayers done. Do we come before one who loved us so much he died for us? And if so, do we stop long enough to hear what he has to say? Please don't run away with the thought now that I have definitely cracked entering God's presence for all time and am a marvellous intercessor now that I have had that experience of hearing God's heart! It is always hard to get to that place of stillness where the Lord has a chance to speak to me. I have personal needs, the needs of the people in my organization... often a whole prayer time can go past without God actually being able to say anything to me!

Our difficulty in getting into the Lord's presence has been called 'The battle of the threshold' because our needs and circumstances drown out his voice and prevent encounter. But we have to get there, because his heart is for rescue – it is far bigger than our little agenda or work for him. If we make it our priority to come before Jesus and his sprinkled blood, he will begin to reveal his heart to us and give us instructions that will change the world around us.

There are times when we come to pray and we find ourselves engulfed by heaviness and we need to do the practical things that free our spirit. Smith Wigglesworth, the nineteenth-century evangelist, is reported to have danced before the Lord for ten minutes each morning, before he did anything else! Singing out our praise, affirming our faith in him by prayer, or speaking out scripture often lifts our spirit so that we can then begin to encounter him and enjoy his conscious presence, rather than just 'say our prayers'. I love the story I heard of the little boy who always resisted going to bed until the very last minute. One day, to his mother's surprise when he was told to go upstairs he went with alacrity! When this persisted for several nights she asked him why he was so eager to go to bed, and her surprise increased when he replied 'It's so that I can say my prayers.'

His mother said 'What do you say to Jesus?'

'I don't say anything', he replied. 'I look at him and he looks at me and we laugh and laugh together!' Now there was someone who had learned what encounter is all about!

During the Hebrides revival, believers waited on God to get clean because they realized that even a speck of sin coming between them and an awesome God would stop his power from falling. As they were praying one night the whole house was shaken; even the cups on the dresser began to rattle! We do not want those things for their dramatic value, but God wants to shake the world and the church today because if we don't let him do it, something else will! Charles Finney, said 'It is as much the duty of the church to bolt from its sleep as it is for fire fighters to awaken when a fire breaks out in the night'.[47] 'Our God is a consuming fire'[48]; when we come to him for cleansing, he will burn up the dross and leave us with the gold of his presence – and then the world about us will begin to rock on its axis. Only God-soaked lives can drench a barren society and change it's landscape.

Esther was someone who was going to be used to change the whole known world at the time, and she spent an entire year just getting clean. So often we somehow feel that because of our faithful service, it is all right to indulge our pet vices. They aren't that bad, after all. So what if work comes before God or family – it is there to provide for both of them isn't it? So what if our language is unholy, everyone else's is, after all. So what if we are economical with the truth, critical of our brothers and sisters... Often our standard is so low that allowing our old strongholds back, criticizing our partner or other people, allowing 'things' to take too great a place in our lives, seem such small offences. But the whole point is that they prevent cleanliness and that prevents access! Esther's skin is *scoured*! If you have been to Africa or India you may have seen how the women at the river will thwack the dirt out of clothes with the use of a stone. It takes ruthless cleansing to fit us for a throne room.

Dave Wilkerson was a young pastor in a rural district, who worked a full day and just had a couple of hours at the end of the day to unwind.[49] One day God asked him for those hours. It was a struggle to give in; he could think of plenty of good reasons why relaxation was important to him, but as a result of his obedience, God's heart for the teenage drug gangs of New York began to beat inside him and 'Teen Challenge' was born out of one man taking the time to encounter. I have a wonderful old leaflet which belonged to my father which has the snappy title *How 25 Great Soul-Winners Were Endued With Power*. It reads like a Who's Who? of great men of faith down through the years. Each one of these men of God got to a place where they knew they needed to enter his presence in a new way, and as a result they began to cry out for the Holy Spirit for service, and he granted their request with world-changing results.

In Hebrews 12 the Lord says he is going to shake everything that can be shaken, and we are in a day where that is beginning to happen. The people of God *will* be shaken, and some will fall. If we do not make the entering of his holy presence our priority, we will have nothing to anchor us in the evil day or to impact our world at what may be one of the most important times in history. We are in such danger today of never going to his place. We sing and dance, receiving healing counsel and wisdom, all of which he died to give us of course. But it is a tragedy never to go to his place or revel in his presence, never having the chance, therefore, to be transformed into his likeness. C.H. Spurgeon was called 'an ugly man made beautiful by the presence of God'!

How is it possible for us to enter the presence on a

regular basis? This really involves nothing new or difficult, nothing that we do not know. First we must give up excuses. We do what we want to do in this life. When I first met my husband I was at full stretch – or so I thought. I had a demanding job, I was running a youth group, and I was seeking to serve God in every way I could. Then I met my husband, and somehow I managed to find two more hours in my day! It was difficult and costly, but I wanted to do it. If I am too busy to communicate in my marriage, what will happen? It is a good marriage, it will not instantly crack up, but the closeness would be gone. It is the same with our relationship with God. I am committed to my marriage, I fight to get quality time with my husband and I have to! Chesterton wrote 'If you leave a thing alone you leave it to a torrent of change. If you leave a white post alone it will soon be a black post'.[50] Loving my husband is easy, maintaining that love is a choice. Loving God is easy, maintaining that love is an hourly, daily, yearly choice. Choice is the first rung of the ladder in Christian discipleship. I have heard (and made!) every excuse in the book, but the truth is still that we do what we want to do!

Hebrews 12:5 says 'See to it that you do not refuse him who is speaking…' If we want to know someone badly we expect to put in the time to get to know them. We will find the time if we want to enough. God is calling people around the world to be set apart for God in our day. The wonderful old evangelist J.H. Jowett wrote this:

> 'Does the world's need pierce the heart and ring even through the fabric of my dreams? I can take my newspaper, which is oftentimes a veritable cupful of horrors, and I can peruse

it at the breakfast table, and it does not add a single tang to my feast. I wonder if one who is as unmoved can ever be a servant of the suffering Lord! ... My brethren, I do not know how any Christian service is to be fruitful if the servant is not primarily baptised in the spirit of a suffering compassion.'[51]

Secondly we must do the practical things that enable this to happen – we make the time practically. Prayer starts with God; he is the one calling us to pray. Every time our mind wanders, instead of feeling guilty, we can thank him for calling us back and carry on. Jesus never rebuked Martha for making the lunch – it was very necessary sustenance – he rebuked her for not working out her priorities. When I was a new Christian if I found my mind wandering I would write my prayers out, and latterly when I am weary I have found this can be the simple means to bring me to a place where I am alert enough in the mornings to hear! We simply have to do whatever it takes to get to that meeting place.

Sometimes when I am speaking about prayer I see peoples' faces become anxious and guilt-ridden, or full of the childlike hope that I will give them a magic formula that will 'crack' prayer open for all time for them! I sometimes say, 'Lucky for you I have got a magic formula for you today, here it is: "just do it!"' In 1 Samuel 1:15–16 Hannah says that she poured out her provocation before God. She got to such a desperate place that she cried out. You may be apathetic today; pour out your apathy then, but begin to speak.

Prayer is contested. John Donne wrote, 'I throw my

selfe down in my Chamber, and I call in, and invite God and His angels thither, and when they are there, I neglect God and His angels for the noise of a flie, for the ratling of a Coach, for the whining of a doore…'![52] Nice to know it isn't just a modern problem, isn't it?! We need to accept it and deal with it in our heart now, making the simple practical choices that enable that to happen. These are things we are taught as new believers, yet which somehow never seem important enough to implement – taking the phone off the hook, ignoring the doorbell, whatever it takes to get time with him. For those who are single parents of small children, we may need to ask God to carve us out spaces in our week, rather than come under condemnation because regular planned times get eroded. But the day of excuses is surely long over, because excuses don't count in wartime. If the church is to take her place as a warrior bride, and receive the riches won for her in blood at Calvary, she needs passionately to repossess her relational inheritance, and stand up in outrage against the one who has stripped her so easily of encounter with her king and bridegroom.

Intercessors often stress the need to put on the armour of God mentioned in Ephesians 6, before every prayer time. As long as this does not become formulaic it is sound practical advice. Ephesians 6:18 indicates that the armour is given for the battle in prayer; surely that is where we come against 'the spiritual forces of this present darkness'? We encounter them every time we choose right from wrong in the workplace, in our social setting, or in the family. We encounter them every time the hungry are fed, the sick healed or the poor raised up. However, we encounter them most potently of all on our knees, and therefore we need to put on our armour if we expect to live to fight another day effectively.

Relationships are not run by formulae! When I was a lot younger I remember reading a hilarious book on marriage relationships which seemed to me completely manipulative. If someone asked my husband why he loved me, I would be outraged if he were to reply that it was 'because she makes good meals each night, cleans the house, walks the dog...'. That would be a functional relationship, not one of love. Yet often when we think about our love for God we are grateful because he performs certain functions for us, he answers our prayers and gives us grace. This is a great start; we know that we enter his courts with gratitude[53] but a relationship cannot grow or deepen when it is only based on function. Only when the precious metal of love, respect and admiration has been deposited in our spirit do we begin to come deeper into his heart.

When my daughter was 3 years old we went to live in a new city. We rented our first house, and at 6pm every night she and I would go outside our house to watch for Daddy. She would stand on the low wall outside the house and watch intently until the familiar figure rounded the corner at the top of the road, and then with a shriek of 'Daddy! Daddy!' she would leap off and sprint down the street so fast that my husband, fearful of a headlong fall, would drop his bag and run to catch her. He said his heart melted every time he saw the little flying figure racing towards him. Jesus said when you pray say 'Abba, Daddy'. He made us for encounter and he made our lives to run on encounter with one who loves us, with a shepherd who leads us, with a holy presence whose light casts a shadow to follow throughout our day.

Jeremiah says 'Let him who boasts, boast of this, that he understands and knows Me'[54]. Intimacy requires concentrating on the character of God. When I was a new believer I sat down one day and wrote out every adjective I could think of to describe God's nature and character. Then I wrote down all the names there were in scripture for Father, Son and Spirit. After that I took one of these names or characteristics every day and meditated on it during my prayer time, noting down insights, thoughts, scriptures or songs that incorporated this attribute, and I spent time worshipping him for this part of his character. The fruit of this was wonderful; not only was I never at a loss for something to praise him for, but through concentrating on him I was learning how to reflect these things in my own character.

Jesus says 'I am the Light of the world'[55], but he also says '*You* are the light of the world'.[56] As the moon reflects the sun, having no light of its own, so we are to reflect the glory of God through mirrored character. As we encounter him we reflect him and our world changes as we ourselves change from one degree of glory to another.

Once we have learned encounter, intercession takes on a very different form. We are not so much praying horizontally, looking at the problems, but praying vertically, looking at one who is more than able to solve them. Jesus, 'in the days of His flesh, [prayed] with loud crying and tears'.[57] He entered into the heart of God in a way that lent passion and desperation to his prayers. Often we feel we cannot be intercessors because we simply don't have that kind of emotion when we come to pray. We say 'I am a baby in the area of prayer', but babies make great pleaders! It never occurs to them that they will not be answered, and so they keep on shouting until they are! We need not to get boxed in by our temperament to one way of praying. Prayer, like every relationship-related thing, is different at different times. Sometimes God just wants us to be with him.

Hebrews 12:28–29 says, 'Since we receive a kingdom that cannot be shaken, let us show gratitude [through our] service with reverence and awe... *for our God is a consuming fire*' (italics mine). When I was working for a church in south-east London we supported a missionary on the Gold Coast. She was a remarkable lady who gave all of her life to serving God and the Africans she had lived with for so long. When she returned on furlough she brought with her some slides, which filled my heart with dread... I had been brought up on missionary slides! But this lady's pictures were different! She showed us a slide where all the Africans were dancing; their faces were shining as they gazed up into the sky. In the top right-hand corner of the slide there was a bright orange mark that looked as though the photograph had been overexposed.

The elderly missionary told us the story behind the picture. One morning, she told us, the missionaries had been woken by loud worship and praise outside in the compound. When they came out they saw all the Africans dancing and worshipping and looking up into the sky. On being asked what they were looking at, the Africans looked puzzled. 'Can't you see them?' they asked. It was the missionaries' turn to be confused. 'See what?' they said. 'The angels,' was the reply, 'God's glory is all around us.' Embarrassingly the missionaries could see nothing! When her photographs came back, our missionary saw immediately the bright orange light in the corner of the picture, where the Africans were facing. Not wanting to exaggerate, she went back to the photographers who had made the prints and asked if it could be produced by overexposure. 'It doesn't look like that,' they replied. 'The sun is coming from the opposite direction. It looks more like the presence of a very bright light!'

Do we want to enter his presence? Do we want to encounter our Father and find the hidden wealth that has been stolen from us for so long? It will cost us. It is not asking God to come to our place but first and foremost it is beginning the ascent to his place. It is telling him that we want to begin to go to a much deeper place, one that will cost us time and tears but a place where we become like him, a place where we receive the great privilege of his heart's burden and begin to learn how to really pray. This may sound a bit heavy for some of us, but I truly believe in our day God is calling his people very seriously to a new place, a place that will shake the heavens and the earth, a place of access to the throne room of the universe. Will you enter?

4

Treasures of Darkness

Gold Extracted from our Wounding

As I was praying one day a scene imprinted itself on my mind. It was of an army walking in the light and moving towards an area of darkness in which whole towns and cities were under enemy captivity. The problem was that a large number of the army were wounded and most of the rest were tending to them. I asked the Lord about the situation and I felt that he said we needed efficiently to train an ambulance unit that could adequately deal with the wounded. The wounded themselves must know that the whole purpose of healing was to get them back on their feet to fight another day. The rest of the army who were left standing needed to know accurately what their part was in the battle. Some were to give active air cover in prayer, some were to take front line positions in terms of evangelism by reaching the culture and generation they find themselves amongst. Others still were to bring supplies, and find their own place of effective service within that fighting unit.

In warfare, civilians can get wounded simply by being in the wrong place at the wrong time, whereas soldiers get wounded because they are in active combat. The wounds may be the same but the reason for being wounded is different. Wounds can be inflicted by the enemy just because we live on a fallen planet. Today many are born already wounded, and it is a messy business if we are going to rescue those in darkness. Then again, wounds can come simply from being part of an army – it would be a foolish soldier who did not know the risk of warfare.

In the next two chapters we are going to look at God's plan for healing, but also at his call to war. If we are not aware that we are constantly in the midst of war, no wonder we can be taken out so easily! We can gain gold from the redeeming of the wounds we have incurred as civilians, as it were, and then we are ready to take the place we were born to adopt, as the bride at war.

One of Hans Christian Andersen's fairytales[58] tells of a demon who created a mirror so warped that everyone who looked into it saw themselves and others as twisted, warped and ugly. One day two apprentice demons stole the mirror and flew high into the air with it, when suddenly it slipped and crashed to earth in millions of tiny fragments. The winds carried these splinters around the world and whenever one got into someone's eye, they saw themselves and others as warped and twisted in some way. There is a lot of truth in the fairy tale! Enemy splinters get into people's eyes through harmful situations, cruel words and deeds and the result is wounding from which we must recover if we can hope to live a life of fullness as God intended.

In the New Testament Jesus is spoken of as Saviour 24 times, but he is spoken of as Lord and King 480 times. We have watered down discipleship nowadays to being about 'me and my happiness', but happiness is a temporary thing related to circumstances, and can be affected by simple occurrences like a rainy day or toothache! God is far less interested in my happiness than my wholeness and my holiness, because those are the solid platform on which to build my life.

In Jesus' manifesto in Luke 4:18, he speaks of coming to set the oppressed free. He is not making a political statement here: in his ministry Jesus raised the fallen who had been damaged in so many ways. If we are going to be followers of Jesus we are meant to be free individuals, or at least coming to freedom.

First we must accept that healing is not always achieved by an instant miracle. Today much money is spent by wounded people trawling meetings for a quick deliverance, a power encounter that will change them forever. The encounter may well happen, but it is not enough! Mark Rutland tells of a member of his congregation who approached him after a morning service in which the speaker had exhorted them to believe for a miracle. This lady and her husband struggled to make ends meet; they both worked long hours and had five children to support, the middle one being severely disabled. She said to her pastor, 'There's a whole lot of days when a miracle just won't do. Miracles only work once, I need something for every day of my life'. Then her face lit up and she said, 'His mercies never end… they are new every morning!'[59] On the days where miracles do not occur, have we found the key to living in mercy?

I remember as a young Christian hearing the story of a small boy who had been told by his brothers that when he went to school he could read comics for himself. He was so excited he was up and ready for school hours beforehand,

and at the end of the day raced home. He threw open his comic book and burst into tears – he couldn't read it! His brothers had not lied to him; he had simply confused promise and process. So much disappointment comes through the childlike hope in us that one day someone will perform an instant miracle and we will be totally healed of the wounds of yesterday. Often there are moments of revelation and healing that do bring miraculous healing, but when we habitually obey fear, lies and authorities that have been set up for many years in our lives, we will need a combination of miracle and mercy. We need revelation from God, a plan of action, and obedience on our part so that the grooves that pain or sin have made may be built up once more.

We will need to commit wholeheartedly to healing, no matter how long it takes. So often we begin the road to wholeness with much joy, but as time goes on things get tough as we start uncovering hidden areas that we have kept secret for years. At this point it is crucial for us not to stop halfway. In Exodus 14:12–15 the Israelites are all for giving up and returning to Egypt (the first of many times). Moses, the man of God, speaks out in faith, 'Stand and see the salvation of the Lord'. This seems to be a winner, but God disagrees, saying, 'Tell the sons of Israel to *go forward*' (italics mine). The only place of safety in following God appears to be in going further out on a limb!

My husband and I worked for many years with students and many of them came from broken and dysfunctional backgrounds. Although we worked and prayed through the pain with many of them, our goal was always to bring them to a place of redemption. Our group called it 'dancing on the ground' – the enemy may have taken a lot of ground in our life but God's intention is to rescue us, to heal us, but not to stop there. Once his healing comes we are to dance on the very ground the enemy took by using it to bring hope to others facing similar despair. Here is the story of one young lady who learned how to dance on enemy ground.

Anna[60] hung her head and looked at the floor. I had to bend closer to hear what she was saying. Her story was of poverty in every area of life. Her father could not read or write and responded to his feeling of inferiority by abuse. Her brother was so ill-treated he had been removed into care. Her mother did love her children but had given up in many social areas and sent them off to school dirty and unkempt with their hair unbrushed. The other school children would call out, 'Here come the paupers!'

But Anna was very bright academically and excelled at school, obtaining a place at university. Her father told her, 'You won't last six weeks!' I met her at the end of six weeks and she was ready to go home, such is the power of negative words. We tried everything to bring healing to her – counselling, care from members of the church, much prayer. Every Sunday night she would come out in tears asking for more prayer and we began to wonder if she could ever be healed.

One night, eighteen months after she had started university, she came out in tears for prayer. It was the end of term and she faced returning home the next day. Jane, a fellow-student, put a hand on her shoulder and began to pray. Suddenly Anna began to run on the spot! I glanced over as I prayed for someone else and was riveted by what I saw. After a little running on the spot she held out what looked like imaginary skirts and twirled in the same direction for about five minutes… there was an army of catchers around her for when she fell through dizziness, but it never happened! She stopped and put her hand up to her hair, in a gesture of brushing, and then sang in a tiny childlike voice, 'I love Jesus, I love Jesus', then the tears flowed and she sat down.

We rushed to her, asking what had happened. She said, 'As soon as Jane said "Come Holy Spirit," I saw myself as a child in a garden. Jesus was playing "tag" with me and I was running away. Then he put a new dress on me. I had never had a new dress and it was blue with lots of petticoats under it, and I was showing them off to him, twirling round and round. Then he brushed my hair, which was tangled, and he said, "I have healed you now, and am sending you to help other children from worse backgrounds than yourself."'

This was not the only miracle that night. Anna's mother, miles away, decided for some reason that she would go to church that evening and she found Jesus the rescuer. Two years later, I had the unspeakable privilege of helping her father to come to Christ, 'Because,' Anna said, 'Jesus loves the abuser as much as the abused.' Anna and her husband reached many in similar places, with the love and hope of a saviour who doesn't just save: he redeems the ground taken by the enemy and makes it fruitful again.'

We will be coming to wholeness until the day we die. We cannot wait until we're 'brand new' before we start to move forward, however a degree of inner healing needs to take place before we do so. It will cost us to get free! It costs to let go of our pet hurts and grievances and self-pity, but as we do, says Isaiah[61], our own light will shine as our story is used to bring healing to the lives of other wounded people.

Our only hope in life is openness and every one of us hates it! But we need it so much. God's plan is for us to become transparent so that people can see through us to Jesus. There is such a relief in transparency, such strain in our lives covering up or pushing things down. True gold is found in letting God into those closed spaces, not just so that we can feel better but so that we can then rescue others who have been similarly imprisoned.

Stop right now and pray, asking God to help you as you do a little exercise. Get a pen and paper and jot down the answers to these questions in five minutes or so (no longer):

- What makes me angry/afraid/anxious or upset/ insecure/defensive?

- Why?

- How do I react outwardly when this happens?

'For though we walk in the flesh, we do not war according to the flesh, for the weapons of our warfare are not of the flesh, but divinely powerful for the destruction of fortresses. We are destroying speculations and every lofty thing raised up against the knowledge of God, and we are taking every thought captive to the obedience of Christ...'[62].

So much is said and written concerning strongholds and fortresses, but we need to define what we mean by those terms. A stronghold or fortress is a wall built around a city to keep people safe from an enemy. The only trouble is that if the enemy is camping around the walls, they keep them prisoner instead. Walls can close around our spirit in various ways.

The enemy, Satan, does not play fair, and he loves to use harmful habit-patterns in our lives, sometimes repeating them down the generations. If members of our family have been involved in the occult, this can certainly reproduce harmful habit patterns from generation to generation, but this is by no means the only way these patterns can be passed down. I knew of one family, all of whom suffered from feeling inferior socially to others in the church they attended. No one else saw them as inferior, and indeed they were universally loved, yet flashes of anger and outbursts of frustration could be seen in three generations of people who were convinced they were perceived as the underdog!

Traumatic incidents, especially in childhood, can equally tie us up and form strongholds from which we need to be freed. Corrie Ten Boom used to say that if we imagine the human spirit to be like a circle, when a traumatic incident occurs to a child it is as though there is a tear in that circle and the enemy can slip in with lies, fear and a host of other 'nasties', to keep us captive. When we come to Christ we change ownership, but will still need healing, much as a faulty car may change ownership but will still need fixing!

Negative words spoken over us can tie us up. When I was small one of my siblings called me 'mentally deficient'. At the time I wasn't entirely sure what that meant but I knew it wasn't good news. I would have told you that those casually-uttered words had never affected me, but when at 18 I didn't receive the mark I had hoped for in an exam, the first words out of my mouth were, 'Well, it's because I am mentally deficient'!

One day a beautiful girl came to see me. She had

just received her doctorate and had been offered a great job yet she felt completely worthless. She spoke of being expelled from her little group of friends at age seven, and feeling different to others from then on. We all know the effects that incidents like these can have on us. Sometimes we react in certain circumstances or with certain people and don't realize the reactions are wrong until the Holy Spirit (or someone else) puts their finger on it. Maybe someone hears from God for us and we come to God to help us, but the Holy Spirit needs access to our feelings. Of course we need to know and choose to live in the love of God during the ordinary grey days. Feelings come and go, but God does want us to experience his love.

The first key to God unlocking our emotions is memory. A friend of mine was taking part in a counselling exercise where she had to introduce herself in the third person. She said, 'This is Helen.[63] She is very uncomfortable doing this kind of thing, she finds it hard to let people see who she really is. She struggles with conflict...' She thought, 'I seriously need prayer!'

We may get a sudden memory. We work it through with a pastor, counsellor or friend and may receive freedom in this area. Once we have brought the memory into the light, repentance may need to take place for the wrong attitudes that our hurt has led us into. We can be oversensitive, bitter and critical or quite the reverse – insensitive, withdrawn or apathetic. The Lord loves us far too much to leave us like this or allow self indulgence in these areas!

We may think, 'Yes, but I go back into that unfair/ painful/unloving situation again. What is the point of being healed if it all happens again?' If we allow Jesus to heal us, hurt will certainly come to us again, but instead of building on all the previous hurts on the inside, it will come to us from outside of our spirit and we will be free to choose to fight, and not to let all the dominoes fall once again. If we are willing to forgive and be made whole God will then give us a plan to live lovingly and creatively in that unfair situation. He will! So often the only person who can keep us in prison (apart from the enemy) is us. Not the circumstances, not the other person. Us.

One young man said to me that all this concentration on wounds was completely introverted, and what we needed was a traditional British 'stiff upper lip'. Now he is wrong and he is right. He's wrong about the stiff upper lip – we stay locked in prison that way. He is right that we are not meant to wallow. Pigs wallow, children of Jesus choose freedom. Listen to God's word through Moses: 'I have set before you life and death, the blessing and the curse. So choose life'![64]

What should we do to free ourselves from strongholds?

By doing the little exercise earlier we may have begun to identify some of the strongholds of habit that keep us chained to a certain set of reactions. Sometimes we discern that our reactions are harmful and we cannot figure out why, and we may need prayer or professional counsel to lead us to understanding. Once we have identified an area in which we need more freedom we need to face Jesus with his question to the leper, 'Are you willing to be made whole?' I heard of a hilarious account of a discussion between some friends who were disabled. What would happen, they wondered, if Jesus were to come by and heal them? Some of them decided that they would rather not be healed by Jesus because they might lose their financial benefits! A similar thing can happen in terms of healing of inner wounds. We might not like ourselves much as we are, but at least it is familiar!

Prayer and deliverance are available for things that have gripped us for many years, but the problem is, that is the easy part! We still have to deal with the far more arduous work of discipleship – the demolition of the stronghold of our habits. We put that wall of habits up, we have to take it down, brick by brick. This is where we start choosing fool's gold often. We can return again and again in search of ministry when what is needed is for us to start deliberately undoing our harmful habits, and moving forward step by painful step. Fool's gold is seen in instant solutions, real treasure is found as we choose to live in the truth, and to speak it out regularly and continuously.

Let us suppose the stronghold we have identified in our life is fear. After we have received prayer, how do we commence demolishing the stronghold? One way is the effective use of scripture: there are 365 verses beginning with 'Fear not...' in the scriptures: one for every day of the year! We can use the scripture as an arsenal of bullets with which to hit the enemy verbally when fearful thoughts arise. Proverbs 18:10 says, 'The name of the Lord is a strong tower; the righteous run to it and are safe'. We need to find and speak out the name of the Lord for every fear that arises.

We need to be practical, naming our fear to someone and taking a practical step in the opposite direction. One young man we knew had had a very bad experience in hospital and had developed a terror of going near hospitals. Before doing further training he got a job and rang to ask me for a reference. 'What's the job?' I asked. 'Hospital porter,' he replied happily. He went on to say that to overcome this fear he needed to do something in the opposite direction, to 'dance on the ground' that God had freed. Who better to care for people who were fearful of the operation they were about to undergo?

Anger is another stronghold that is hard to overcome. When my daughter was little I tried to explain that she needed to deal with anger rightly, not to let it fly, nor to suppress it. She looked at me seriously and said, 'Let me see if I've got this right. When someone makes me angry, I mustn't hit back because that would hurt God. I mustn't push it down or the anger will burst out and hurt somebody else. So when I am angry, I need to go into the toilet, shut the door and tell Jesus I'm angry until it's finished!' A pretty good solution, I've always thought!

Once we have identified a stronghold, we need to admit sin where necessary. There is a saying that 'hurt people hurt people'. It is true. Many of our sinful reactions have come through someone else's misuse of us but the reactions are still sin and must be named as such! Anna, who encountered Jesus so dramatically was still tempted by old habits of self-pity, and she would not be healed today if she had not determined to take down the remains of that stronghold herself. The Lord cannot make us whole while we are still excusing sin or blaming it on others in the past.

We may have something we need to renounce. I received a sixteen-page letter from someone once apologizing for how 'useless' she was. I had in fact thought this girl was one of the stars of the outreach we were doing so the letter came as a shock. I asked her when she had started to feel useless and for her there was a specific incident that she could recall, when she was tiny. She was in the street, walking with her mother and her mother called her useless. Sometimes a spoken word can enter us like a curse and lodge there, and this is what had happened. I encouraged the young lady to pray a prayer of renunciation which went something like this:

'Lord, I renounce the enemy and all that he has done in my life. In Jesus' name I reject the hold he has in my life in the area of uselessness [you can insert whatever is bothering you instead]. His authority over my mind was broken at the cross and rendered powerless. Right now I take back every place where I have colluded with the enemy by entertaining lies concerning my uselessness and bring all my thoughts under Jesus' lordship. Amen.'

We will still have freedom contested, and if we are to be a warrior bride we are to expect attack. First of all we will receive attack from the enemy of course, who does not want to lose ground in our lives. We will need to be accountable to someone whom we can phone any time, someone who will cover us in prayer and keep us focused when we are tempted to go back into old habits. These are habits we may have had for many years. We need to say, 'No matter what it takes or how long this takes, I am going to overcome this stronghold in Jesus. Secondly, we are going on the attack against the gates of hell – we take this ground fighting.

There are two particular areas in terms of inner

freedom which are recurring strongholds in our generation and in which we often choose fool's gold instead of coming to God for the hidden wealth from his treasury.

The first is in the area of sexual freedom. Today everywhere we go there are explicit materials, and it is very hard for the child of God to stay clean. There is a tendency, therefore, for gross unreality to grow up in the church of God. We talk about purity often but there is little grass roots acknowledgement and radical dealing with this area, and this leads to darkness and secrecy which will cripple our walk with God and our relationships with one another. The word 'occult' means 'hidden', and Satan lives in hidden places created by secrets.

The only answer for us is for a hold in this area to be broken. It is best that one, preferably more than one person knows – wouldn't it be great if, when we met together we could just say, 'Could you pray for me – I am struggling with temptation', with no one thinking the worse of us? After all, which of us is immune to temptation? We start by telling one or two people who will be faithful to us. Accountability means faithful prayer, and loving follow-up if we are to help one another to walk closely with God over these issues.

If we have habits of pornography it is good to pray with a leader to make sure any demonic stronghold is broken. If we have accumulated pornographic books or magazines we need to burn them and decide what to spend our money on instead. Where internet pornography is concerned, we can take advantage of computer programs such as 'Covenant Eyes', which will alert your friend's computer immediately if you log onto a pornographic site. Pornography is an enormous issue for today's church and many struggle with guilt, not feeling able to confess and get clean because they do not feel they will be able to resist again. One young man I knew asked his mother to be his internet covenant keeper – you really must be serious about it if you will go to such lengths!

2 Corinthians 10:5 talks about taking thoughts captive. It is helpful for us to decide what time of day, or in what circumstance we are most vulnerable, mentally and emotionally, and to take advantage of the many creative ways of 'taking our thoughts captive', either practically getting up and making a cup of coffee, or choosing to worship. Some find it helpful to take a scripture, write it out and place it by the bed so that as soon as our thoughts go down that route we grab them and turn them to God's word, learning it, reading it, praying it. We can take the scripture in our pocket during the day. Our thought life may slip a few times, but generally if we keep taking our thoughts captive courageously, after a day or two the ferocity of that mental assault will lift. One young man came to see me concerning a struggle with lustful thoughts. I talked with him about taking his thoughts captive and being accountable to others, prayed with him and he left. Nearly a year later he came to see me with the same questions. I asked, 'Did you take your thoughts captive as we discussed?' His face lit up. 'Oh yes, it was great,' he said. 'So why are you back asking the same questions?' I asked him.

He looked a little sheepish. 'Well I was just wondering,' he said tentatively, 'Is there might be an easier way?'

Fool's gold is easily acquired, but wealth from the King's purse will last a lifetime. It is acquired by regular obedience and choice. There is no instant solution to strongholds, we take them down brick by brick, but while we will be tempted all our life in one way and another, regular choice to obey brings a renewed mind, freedom and joy.

The second recurring stronghold in our generation is the area of self-image. In our postmodern age, 'how I feel' is the arbiter of what I do and say. If I am at the centre of my universe, no wonder I have a crisis in terms of image! I was asked to speak in a university bar on the topic of image. The meeting was laid on by the Christian Union and I did not think many outsiders would attend. How wrong could I be? The place was packed! Image is a subject everyone wants to know about, from the anxious teenager to anyone involved in party politics!

Because we need to be acceptable, there is a real overemphasis on looking just right, which in turn spawns materialism, and an obsession with getting just the right look, home, or social grouping. Of course getting just the right image can divorce us from the reality of who we are, making a schism that can threaten to overturn us. Young people (and the not-so-young) begin to hate themselves, as the pressure mounts, evidencing itself in mutilation, self-criticism and lack of confidence which in turn leads to a lack of genuine friendships. How can I genuinely care for the other person when I am absorbed with the question 'What are they thinking about *me*?' And of course a rickety self-image leads to a lack of trust in God. If I know that he is my creator and loving Father and I look in the mirror (or at my gifts or circumstances) and am revolted or disappointed, how will I trust him for the big questions of life?

It is tragic when this is to be found in the bride but

of course it is, as far too often we reflect our society. We can start to overcome the tyranny of image by accepting responsibility for where we are now, and by renouncing the grip the enemy has on our life in the area of poor image. I have known people (including myself) completely conquer this area – it takes time and continuous obedience to speak out truth, but God has a plan for his redeemed bride. She is to be so aware of her beauty and desirability to him that she is freed in confidence to look beyond herself to his world.

In my own life a change in the area of self-image began by my learning how to thank God for his intricate choice and design of me. The Lord taught me an amusing lesson around this time. As a child I had envied my mother's big grey eyes and wished I had been given them instead of my rather boring brown ones! Later, in my twenties, I worked for a church, and was called out to visit someone involved in witchcraft (some of her story is told in the next chapter). After she had come to Christ, one day she said, 'You know why I asked you in that first day? I never asked Christians in, but you had red hair and brown eyes, just like me! Most redheads have blue or grey ones!' I laughed all the way home, acknowledging that God does do all things well!

The psalmist says in Psalm 139 that we were intricately and carefully designed in our mother's womb. There are things we can change, but in the case of those we cannot, we take time to thank him for those things we have found hard to accept. I have found that as we say, 'If I cannot change this, it must be his choice for me', peace comes in to the place of discontent. Anger and resentment send us into prison; looking for affirmation by getting the right clothes or friends or circumstances will lead to fool's gold. But a choice to give thanks opens us up to what God is going to do and brings the untold wealth of confidence and peace from God's eternal riches. In Ephesians 2:10 we read that 'we are His workmanship'. The word in Greek for 'workmanship' is *poema* from which we get the word 'poem'. You are a piece of poetry God is writing, and the great news is that he isn't finished yet!

There is often a time factor in emotional healing. Fortunately things surface at different times or we would be overwhelmed. We can bring the hurt to Jesus and he can remove the blockage instantly, but it may take a while for us to learn to live in freedom. Our immature reactions will change as we constantly choose what the old hymn calls the 'gold of obedience'[65], and we will walk into freedom rather than accept the pyrite of emotional highs and lows that keep us enslaved.

In the West our culture has changed from modernism, where people sought a rational scientific explanation for everything, to postmodernity where the emotions have far greater importance. When the modernist mindset invaded the church this meant that the Holy Spirit and works of power were regarded with suspicion. People relied more and more on the mind, and rational explanations were found for spiritual power. We were conducting a student meeting one Sunday and a girl was there who had broken a bone in her wrist on the preceding Friday. X-rays were taken of the bone, she had a cast put on her wrist and arm and was sent home, still in pain. On the Sunday night we all prayed for her that God would reduce the pain. A few minutes later she interrupted the worship to say she thought God had healed her, as she had felt warmth go right down her arm. I have to admit I was not as filled with as much delight as I might have been as her arm was in plaster and I could see no way of telling if she was healed!

The following morning the girl called me to say she was going to the university medical centre to have the cast taken off. Still full of faith, I suggested she wait a day or two! She went, however, and received more discouragement: she must keep the cast on for six weeks, they said. She called me again and said that she was going to the hospital next! As she was normally a quiet, shy girl, I was beginning to have a little faith that all this persistence meant she really had been healed. At the hospital one nurse said, 'I do believe in prayer, but not for broken bones', but she must have impressed them, because when the doctor came he said that the cast was put on badly and they would take it off and reset it. You've guessed it – her wrist was completely healed! The doctors professed themselves amazed at this; her non-Christian friends at university were very excited at the story. The church? After she had given her testimony, people came up to me, saying, 'Grace, did *you* see the X-rays? I mean, God doesn't do that kind of thing!' Insisting on a rational explanation for everything has sometimes closed our minds to the super-rational (not irrational) working of Christ in our lives.

When Western culture became postmodern, the question 'How do I feel?' took centre stage. The mind dominates modernism and the emotions dominate postmodernism; and between the two falls the will. It is our will that determines whether or not we are going to choose freedom.

If we are going to be free we will have to deal, sooner or later, with the whole issue of our emotions. Some of us have them locked up tightly for fear of what might come out. Others of us are completely subject to our emotions. Inner freedom means we are in control but free to express the emotional life God gives us.

An old song by Graham Kendrick had these words:

> *Now I can laugh and I can cry and I can sing,*
> *The sweetest joys and saddest tears can now begin,*
> *An honest heart and honest eyes,*
> *It's been a beautiful surprise,*
> *Since God gave me my true feelings.*[66]

Once the Lord has access to our emotions he gives us authority over them. I have a friend who has been for many years in a violent situation. She could have chosen to take herself out of it many times and some would argue that she should have done. However, she has chosen to stay and many times we have prayed for God to release forgiveness and grace in her to go back to choose to love those who have harmed her. Gradually God has brought change and healing in the situation and the people concerned, as she has constantly taken authority over her emotions and chosen the painful path of forgiveness and love.

We choose, likewise, to be close to God. At some points this is easy, of course, but on many occasions we have to choose. I am not very alert in the early morning and if my husband is hoping for intense hearts and flowers when leaving for work, he might well be waiting for some time! However, that does not prevent me from kissing him goodbye in the morning and talking to him about the day. The choice and commitment to love is what keeps that closeness alive, far more than emotional fits and starts.

It is similar with our choice to be close to Jesus and close to people. Repeating loving habits sustains the emotions of love rather than the other way round. We can live like a child of God even when our emotions are in the pit, by learning the habits of thanksgiving which sustain us all our life. Choice brings the 'solid joys and lasting treasure'[67] rather than fool's gold which evaporates with our mood swings.

Increasingly the twenty-first century church needs to see these choices as an obedience and a warfare issue as we become free to take authority over our life instead of being ruled by our emotions. If I do not submit my will to Jesus I may do something to hurt the Lord. My mind will tell me it is wrong, my emotions will feel remorse, but nothing will happen until God gets access to my will. Obeying God, whether I feel like it or not, sets my will free. The more I obey, the more I am in control and able to choose; the less I obey, the less I am in control and able to choose.

When I was a new Christian I remember someone talking about what 'new life' really meant. He said something along these lines: 'Imagine that when you were born a tape was switched on, and onto that went everything that makes you you. Your thoughts, encounters, relationships, everything goes onto that tape. Then one day you become a Christian. What happens to the tape?'

'It gets erased,' we all said dutifully.

'Really?' he replied. 'Then you will all have amnesia! You won't know who you are! No, what happens is that you are given a new tape onto which you record the reactions of your new life in Christ. The only problem is that the old tape is longer than the new one, so it is far easier to switch into the old habit patterns. In God's grace the more often we choose the gold, the longer our new tape will become so that it becomes more and more habit-forming.'

In John 4, in the story of the woman at the well, Jesus perfectly demonstrates God's method of restoration for wounded people. The first thing we see from this story is that sometimes past pleasure needs releasing. When things get tough, many of us live with our head turned to look over our shoulder. 'It used to be so nice when....' The woman at the well might well have had nostalgia for a time when people talked to her as though she actually mattered. The Lord was going to give her living water, but it would have been no use if she stayed looking backwards.

I had been praying with someone for some time concerning abuse issues in her past. God had done a lot of healing in her, and one day as we were finishing a time of prayer together I had a mental picture of Jesus standing at the gate of a field in which a little girl was dancing. He was unmistakably pointing out of the field, gesturing for her to move on. She looked at me and said, 'That is so accurate. When I was abused I made a mental note that I never wanted to grow up beyond the age I was on the day before it all happened.' The Lord was saying 'Now is the time for you to let go of past good times and begin to live in today'.

Luke 17:32 has only three words in it: 'Remember Lot's wife'! She, along with Lot and their two daughters, had been saved out of an awful situation, but she simply would not let go of the past and it calcified her. She was literally immobilized.

If I asked someone when they came to Christ they might give me the date or time of their conversion and we would know what they mean. But the Bible usually uses the present continuous tense when the Greek verb 'to save' is used – we are being saved. I am not a very good swimmer, and if I were swimming in the sea and got out of my depth it would be serious. Imagine the air-sea rescue heard of my plight and sent out a helicopter. I would be thrilled as the rope came down and I adjusted it under my arms. 'Hurrah, I'm saved!' I would think. But if after several hours I was still dangling under the helicopter I would be less joyful! I would have been saved *from* the sea, but not *to* land. So many people feel they have been saved *from* death but not *to* vital everlasting life. For some of us, entering that life may start with a choice to let go of the past.

We have looked at the fact that past wounding can be redeemed. The woman at the well has a lot to mark her out as wounded. She is a woman (a rabbi in Jesus' time once said, 'I would rather teach my dog than a woman'). She is a despised Samaritan, she has been an object to men and probably rejected by women (she is at the well at noon, far too hot a time for the women of the city to draw water). Superficially this lady is flippant, she cannot let him too close, but she is thirsty, and that is what Jesus addresses. The wonderful wealth we need to grasp here is that Jesus wants to heal our wounds but that is not all. Who does the woman go to? The passage tells us she goes to 'the men of the city'[68]. Imagine their chagrin when she runs to them, shouting, 'He knows!' If she had not had her particular past, numbers of men would not have streamed out to the Saviour that day. It does not rejoice his heart when we have sinned in the past or suffered pain, but he will take that very pain, once healed, and use it – not one tear will be wasted! It is wonderful to see God take the very things that have hurt us and use them as the building blocks of hope in others' lives. Redemption is the most valuable treasure we can ever find, after God himself!

King David suffered from failure at different times of his life. Never more so than when he arranged the effectual murder of one of his own 'mighty men' because he had slept with this man's wife and got her pregnant. God confronts David, he is disciplined and repents. But that is not the end of it. Much later one of David's sons rapes Tamar, one of the royal princesses, and David fails to discipline him. The girl's brother, Absalom, plans and executes the murder of this young man. Although David distances himself from Absalom, again he does not punish this deed. Why? Because he has not learned that past failure can be forgiven. Our own failures, if they have not received thorough healing as well as forgiveness, will lead to weakness in our walk with God. David paid dearly for not facing up to his failures in such a way that he could be free to make righteous judgments later. The sense of failure is a very persistent stronghold. There is such stress caused in the Christian church (and among Christian workers, too!) in needing to 'be OK'. Sometimes we fail, we may be forgiven but we need to be healed – we are part of Jesus' victory, we sign our name next to his on the victory document written at Calvary.

Finally, past disappointment can be transformed. The Authorized Version says 'Hope deferred maketh the heart sick'[69] ... it certainly doth! That woman must have had many disappointments in her life, but she dumped her pathetic little water pot and ran forward. There wasn't just a trickle available to her that day, there were rivers to flow out of her inmost being.[70] Jesus was going to redeem her past.

Let's allow Jesus to ask us the question 'Will you be made whole?' Sometimes we have to struggle through to a 'Yes', in obedience to his desires for us. We need to admit sin, receive prayer or counsel, plan a course of action. But most importantly of all, we must choose to go for gold! As we make it our deepest desire to let Jesus into those places where we have been held captive, he will lift us up on our feet, so that we can become a 'restorer of streets in which to dwell'.[71]

5

Warrior Bride

Choosing the Battle

'Be kind, for everyone you know is facing a great battle.'

Philo of Alexandria

'The secret to success in warfare is no to be found in giving your life for your country, but in seeing to it that the enemy gives *his* life for *his* country.'

General George S. Patton

Surprisingly little attention is paid to the fact that we are at war. Of course people can be embarrassingly dramatic about spiritual warfare and see the enemy under every bush, but really this is a paltry excuse for missing our calling as a soldier.

There are many clues in the New Testament as to why Jesus came: 'The Son of Man did not come to be served, but to serve'[72], 'I came that they may have life, and have it abundantly'[73], '…to save that which was lost'[74], 'I come to cast fire upon the earth'[75]. One reason for Jesus' coming to earth is found in 1 John 3:8: 'The Son of God appeared for this purpose, to destroy the works of the devil'. In the Old Testament we find characters like Daniel who stir up major attack against themselves, as a direct result of serving God passionately. On the whole we the church are no longer a warrior bride and there are a number of reasons for this.

In the previous chapter we looked at the fact that today, in the West particularly, there is so much wounding that much of the army are in the hospital wing either receiving or giving ministry to the wounded. This is desperately necessary, but what is often missing is the understanding that the goal of healing is to put the wounded back into life in all its fullness, to fight another day! As we saw in the previous chapter, a few decades ago our culture was modern with an emphasis on the mind and the material, and we became uncomfortable with the idea that there was such a thing as a spiritual battle going on for the people's souls. With the advent of a postmodern culture, personal comfort and the 'feel-good factor' have entered the equation, an outlook which is incompatible with a time of war. The end result is that the bride often enjoys a quiet life, remaining undisturbed and pampered, without any idea that a battle is quietly and inexorably being lost.

C. Peter Wagner writes:

'I wish we didn't have to think about this phase of ministry as "warfare"… If I personally were to choose an analogy for our struggle with the enemy, I might want to say it is like a football game. I could think of many very descriptive parallels between football and our adversarial relationship with Satan. This would be much more pleasant than talking in militaristic terms... But, unlike football, our spiritual struggle bears eternal consequences. It can mean the difference between heaven and hell for millions of people. Warfare is not a game. *There is a finality to war unlike any other human activity.*[76] [Italics mine.]

Once I was approached by a German student who wanted to make a commitment to Christ. She said to me, 'The only problem I have is that I don't believe in the devil'.

'That's fine,' I assured her. 'It is not mandatory to believe in the devil in order to come to Christ. But if you live the life Jesus calls you to, you will certainly become aware of the devil very quickly!' And so it transpired!

The disturbing thing is that if we are not aware of being in a war, we are not living the life Jesus lived. It is as simple as that. Jesus brought intense confrontation with the forces of darkness wherever he went, because of who he was. This might have taken the obvious guise of the demonic erupting when he appeared, or the far more subtle route of legalism, but opposed he was – every time! The bride of Christ is to reflect his character. Therefore it stands to reason that who we are should provoke confrontation with the powers of darkness.

Jesus opposed the enemy by *his words* – he challenged religious double standards and injustice in such a way that there were attempts on his life well before he went to the cross. He opposed the enemy by *his works*, raising those whose social status or disability precluded them from enjoying abundant life. He also opposed the devil by *his wonders*... whenever the sick were healed, the demonized delivered or the dead raised, the works of the evil one were destroyed. We preach a watered-down version of the gospel at our peril. Much of our preaching portrays Jesus as a gentle, caring man, universally loved, and for some it is a mystery as to why he was ever put to death! The real Jesus leaps out of the pages of scripture, whip of cords in hand in the temple, confronting the evil one in the desert, refusing the double standards of the Pharisees, fiercely loving and challenging the disciples. Who Jesus was and is always produces conflict.

If we are living a life that is full of his Spirit and world-changing (and that is the call of discipleship), then we will also provoke opposition. This is not a mandate to be as obnoxious as we can be, it is simply saying that power always provokes opposition. It is no surprise that as soon as the Holy Spirit begins to work powerfully in a congregation or an individual, opposition rises. Seen correctly, opposition is the enemy's vote of confidence in us that we are beginning to live Jesus-lives. One invaluable test of our life or ministry is to ask the question 'What is under attack in my life at the moment?' Clearly the enemy sees this as the important area to go for.

On that great final day when Jesus returns, there will be no smell of cordite in the air. 2 Thessalonians 2:8 says that he will simply breathe out. Creation was made by his breath and on the last day Jesus will breathe out and the enemy will be no more. That is total authority. It is important that we are well taught concerning our part in the battle and it is important that we commit as a soldier. Soldiers may die, unfair things do happen to the people of God. We commit those we love into the hands of Jesus daily, covering them in prayer, then we leave the consequences of war to him. War is an activity that only a few sick people actually enjoy; it is something we commit to because it is totally necessary for the rescue of anguished people.

General Patton said: 'No sane man is unafraid in battle, but discipline produces in him a form of vicarious courage.'[77] Just as the Lord interferes in human affairs so Satan ('the enemy', as Jesus calls him) seeks to twist and maim and destroy. We see this in large evil regimes and ideologies and we see it in our own and others' lives. In C.S. Lewis's brilliant book *The Screwtape Letters*, the older demon Screwtape instructs his nephew Wormwood:

'My dear Wormwood

I note with displeasure that your patient has become a Christian... One of our great allies at present is the Church itself. Do not misunderstand me. I do not mean the Church as we see her spread out through all time and space and rooted in eternity, terrible as an army with banners. That I confess is a spectacle which makes our boldest tempters uneasy. But fortunately it is quite invisible to these humans. All your patient sees is the half-finished sham-gothic erection on the new building estate. When he goes inside, he sees the local grocer with rather an oily expression on his face bustling up to offer him one shiny little book containing a liturgy which neither of them understands...'[78]

How easy we make it for the enemy to sow cynicism!

If we pray for revival we are asking for war. A church standing as a viable alternative to pornography, to the occult, to all the plagues affecting our society at present, is asking for major conflict. Queen Esther stood out from all that was on offer, and as a result her life was under threat. We are not to fear, we signed up for war and if we do not step outside the circle of God's protection, whatever comes he will work for good.

I discovered the reality of warfare at the start of my Christian ministry. During my first job as a pastoral assistant in a church in south London, I was sent to visit a girl who had been initiated into witchcraft. She was not interested in speaking about Jesus, and said she was seeking to do good in her own way, which included contacting God through witchcraft. But she was lonely and I continued to visit her as a friend.

One day when I arrived she practically fell on my neck begging for help. She had been ill for several weeks and her first words to me were 'Thank goodness you've come, please help me!' To my surprise I found myself saying, 'I can't, I'm afraid. The only thing I have to offer you is Jesus and you say that what you are doing is pleasing to him.' She said, 'Not any more! Yesterday I had a vision of Jesus, shining and beautiful, and immediately I knew the difference between who he is, and what I am doing.'

'The Son of God appeared for this purpose, to destroy the works of the devil'[79]. It is a revelation of Jesus that destroys the enemy's works. That time many years ago has given me a conviction that Jesus is far mightier than the evil one, but also, that the enemy never gives up. Even when a battle has been won by an invading force, there is often a resistance army which continues to fight, to destroy communications, and it does win some rounds.

Early in our marriage my husband and I rang our pastor when everything seemed to be going wrong with our plans. He listened to our garbled account of recent events and I have never forgotten his reply : 'We are in a war and the enemy does win some battles, but God is the master chess player who turns all to his advantage.'

This is hard and painful for those of us who have lost loved ones, or who feel wounded in the struggle, but it is nevertheless true. When Jesus was approached by John the Baptist's disciples, he was asked an agonized question posed by the imprisoned John. 'Are you the coming one, or shall we look for someone else?' John may well have been feeling 'If he is the Messiah, why am I not set free?' Jesus' reply is significant: 'Go and report to John what you hear and see: the blind receive sight and the lame walk, the lepers are cleansed and the deaf hear, the dead are raised up and the poor have the gospel preached to them. And blessed is he who does not take offence at Me.'[80]

Why is this significant? It is because Jesus is quoting directly from the messianic prophecy in Isaiah 61:1... with one notable omission. He leaves out the phrase 'to proclaim liberty to captives and freedom to prisoners' – and John was in prison. There are times in our lives where specific promises in scripture are not true in our present circumstances and the evil one whispers 'There you are! I told you it wasn't true, or if it is, it's not true for you because you don't matter to God'. It is at times like this that we win the battle by simply remaining upright, in the evil day, and refusing to stumble despite the pain of war.

Faced by obvious major warfare most of us will 'go

up a gear'. Something happens and we suddenly wake up to the fact that we are at war. In one sense relief can come when we realize we are not just a terrible Christian, we really are in a battle! If we have any sense we pocket our pride and get some friends together to pray and support us when we feel under specific attack. However, the attacks that are hardest are those which are insidious. Maybe we have become low and tired, a number of disappointments build up, we keep shrugging them off – and then something good at last seems about to happen, we allow ourselves to hope, and the rug gets pulled from under us.

It is at a times of disillusionment like this, rather than in the huge and obvious battles, that everything simply crashes round our ears and we can lose a lot of ground in our spirit by colluding with the devil's lies. A frequent lie is 'You don't matter. Not to God. Not to anyone'. We come to a place where we feel that God will never smile on us again. As Adrian Plass brilliantly puts it in his *Letter to Lucifer*:

> 'The thing is, Lucifer, … I know now why you are so bitterly, cruelly determined to prevent as many as possible from finding peace. It's because you've lost it, isn't it? You wanted more than it's possible to have, and you lost everything. Jesus will never smile at you again, and all that's left is to suck others into the loveless vacuum that you inhabit.'[81]

Most of us are familiar with the devil's tactics to stop us doing the Lord's work. As people prepare to go out in mission, I have seen every variation of opposition and obvious assault upon them, ranging from an attack on their health or their parents' health, family disapproval or break-up, money problems, old sinful strongholds, or a new relationship promising much but with the price tag that they give up their calling. The list is endless.

There are many traps set for unwary travellers. The first is always pride, the chief of sins and the one through which the enemy fell in the first place. Someone said, 'When you start out in the Christian life the enemy whispers "You'll never make it", but if you stay long enough he comes back and says, "You've made it now"'! We live in a culture which is totally self-centred and therefore reflecting the chief characteristic of the 'God of this world'. We detect pride in unusual places in our lives – in areas where we used to be teachable, we suddenly have everything to teach and nothing to learn. I remember many years ago hearing someone say that humility is listening to a sermon on something we know well, and still being able to learn from it! At other times people praise our gifting, and while we deprecate, we begin to live more and more for applause. A simple question I often ask myself is, 'When did the Holy Spirit last rebuke me, and did I respond?'

Most of us are aware that there can be a spiritual dynamic in certain areas which affects people living there whether they are Christians or not. One missionary said to me that in the early days of living in the country she was very aware of the ruling spirit of the area which caused people so much trouble. However, the longer she lived there the less she noticed it. There has long been a debate as to whether Christians should 'pray against the spirit of the area', and there is no guidance in scripture concerning this. Personally I find it easier to pray *for* something rather than against it, so once I identify what the enemy seems to be doing in an area I seek to pray and live in the opposite spirit.

It is important not to treat something as far-fetched because a few people overreact. I visited a country some years ago where the divorce rate was said to stand at 98 per cent. Tragically we heard of a number of missionary couples who had gone out to minister in that place whose own marriages then broke up. They were not well enough protected through the prayers of those sending them, and through recognizing the spiritual atmosphere of the place where they were in ministry. We do not need to fear, we need to do what any soldier would do – make a careful reconnaissance of the area we live in and arm ourselves accordingly.

Like soldiers in ancient times, we need to guard against having a rusty sword! Ephesians tells us that the sword of the Spirit is the word of God. In *The Lion, the Witch and the Wardrobe*, after Peter's first encounter with the enemy, Aslan says to him, 'Son of Adam... whatever happens, never forget to wipe your sword'.[82] Unbelievably, this is one of today's most frequent downfalls amongst Christians and Christian workers alike. In days past people would know and use the word of God, and seek to meet with God, even if they got duty and delight a bit mixed up!

Let's wake up! What is the first aim of enemy attack in warfare? As we saw earlier, it is to disrupt communications with central command, and to cut off food and water supplies. Prayer and finding God in his word are not only necessary to a love relationship, they arm us for battle and therefore they are not simply an option, they are essential. Today the church leader fears to say that if work squeezes out quality prayer and knowledge of scripture, something is wrong. There is such fear that people will fall back into legalism and 'duty', and must never be told what to do, only given an option. It seems to make far more sense to choose these things because they are essential to our relationship with Jesus, and for our personal survival! When did a general addressing the army, about to encounter the enemy's worst, say, 'Well, troops, I don't want you to feel you *have* to fire if you're too busy'? When did the Home Guard in the Second World War say, 'We encourage you only to use the blackout if you feel like it'? We have absorbed the culture of our day so deeply that the urgency of scripture is lost. And what does scripture say? That is exactly how it's going to be in the last days!

One of the reasons our sword can become rusty is that we can begin to love the work we do for him more than the Lord himself. Without noticing this can happen to all of us and the fact that the scripture calls this idolatry certainly passed me by for many years. We get less and less time to spend with our Commander because of all there is to do, and as a result, our spirit dries up even though the work may still be exciting. This is a place of intense danger – we will not spot the enemy's tactics because communication has been cut off, and eventually we will have serious famine.

Amos 8:11 speaks of a 'famine of the word of the Lord', and we in the West are in danger of living in that day! Paul speaks to Timothy of a coming day when people want, and receive, sermons that please them, and the result will be that they start believing in myths. We are to beware of fool's gold in this area. Helpful as many courses are to us there comes a day when we must begin to put them into practice. This is always a lot less exciting and more backbreaking (and often heartbreaking) than opting for another course!

In a war, the clever deflection of our focus can be lethal. Materialism often trips us up without our noticing it. I have the privilege of visiting many countries which are time rich and cash poor, and often the Christians in these countries have time and space to devote to things that they think are most important. For us it is difficult to find ways to get off the treadmill, yet we need to devote time and prayer to working through this issue with God rather than simply giving it up as impossible. A recurring theme in scripture is our position as 'sons of Abraham'. Throughout the Bible people of faith have taken steps to live for what matters eternally. Abraham himself left a very civilized culture where they had piped underfloor heating, in Chaldea, to live in a tent. You notice wherever he went he pitched tents and built altars, showing what he considered permanent and what was temporary. It takes an act of violence and of faith to throw away fool's gold and invest in eternity, yet it will free us up to spend our lives on what counts.

As a child I remember watching a thriller where the hero was captured and repeatedly woken from sleep in order to weaken his defences. Exhaustion is a very simple tool of the enemy to keep us from abundant living and effective warfare. The pace of life and the demands of work, family and church can send the sanest of us under from time to time! I remember my doctor once looking me in the eye and saying kindly but firmly, 'You probably aren't being as effective as you think you are, you know!' I needed to hear it. I was so busy trying to save the world that I was slowly shrivelling up in spirit and every day seemed to be a weary round of activity before I could sink back under the covers.

In 1 Kings 19, we find Elijah, who had been initially obedient and had seen a real and dramatic victory for God's name, suddenly fall prey to exhaustion and fear. God does not rebuke him at this vulnerable point in his life. He gives him what he badly needs: food and sleep. The rebuke only comes later when Elijah is tempted to stay in a self-pitying, self-justifying hole rather than moving on. Some of us are true perfectionists, and the enemy sees that instead of stopping us from serving God, he can push us too far and then leave us in a morass of guilt. We need to take time to let God minister to us when we are exhausted, and when we are ready to move off again, we need to obey his call and learn from our mistakes rather than letting them paralyse us from ever moving again!

Perhaps two of the most effective of all the enemy's traps for the bride of Christ are not always easily spotted. The first of these is disappointment. Disappointment is the death of faith. Something we have hoped would happen falls through, some promise is unfulfilled and though outwardly we may still be standing, inwardly we have stepped back. Once we recognize where we have got to spiritually, the only answer I have found is to be honest with God and to admit disappointment, to confess unbelief, and in spite of our feeling of vulnerability, to risk again. No war was ever won, no true wealth ever attained, without setbacks and the choice to risk again.

Broken relationships often prove to be by far the most damaging attack on Christ's body here on earth. Before church missions there are physical and material disasters but the most effective attack is against relationships within a team. Criticism strikes a nail into Christ's body here on earth, that is why unity is essential. The truth is we do not do all that it takes to preserve loving relationships. Sometimes we simply cannot clear something up with someone even though we try, and we have to pray that reality will break through in God's time for us. But that is not repentance and restoration. We need to try everything we know to put things right, because we can only truly move on where there is reality coupled with a choice to forgive.

The story is told of a large successful church in Czechoslovakia, just before Russia invaded in 1968. There were five elders who led the church and the enemy managed to use suspicion and distrust to break relationship amongst the leaders. The church split apart, each of the elders taking a section with them, but one elder could not bear what had happened and he returned time and again to each of the others begging for reconciliation. This did not happen easily; it is hard to trust someone again when they have hurt you, and it does not come overnight. But with the grace of God, reconciliation was made and the church was reunited. Then the Russian tanks rolled in to Prague and all five of the church leaders were arrested and put in solitary confinement. An interrogator went round to each, sowing lies in order to get information from them. He would begin: 'You know what your brother said about you…?' and proceed to spread damaging gossip concerning the prisoner. His amazement grew as time after time each man replied, 'I do not believe my brother would say that about me, but if he did, I forgive him'! In the end the interrogator called them all into a room together and asked them how they could trust each other so implicitly.

They told him a story of brokenness, of failure, and of restoration, until he fell on his knees and asked for mercy from the one who reconciles. If we are to be a warrior bride we cannot afford to be the fractured, embittered army that we are in so many places, moving from church to church each time we fall out with someone.

Mark 11:25 is a difficult scripture! There really is no way round it. 'Whenever you stand praying, forgive, if you have anything against anyone, so that your Father who is in heaven will also forgive you your transgressions.' There is so much to say on this subject (and Jesus has a lot to say about it), but let us establish some simple principles. This verse does not say, 'if you are really bitter and twisted, forgive', or 'if you are not justified in hating this person, forgive'. It says, 'if you have anything against anyone'. You cannot even get away with saying, 'I just have a chemical reaction to them, I avoid them because I find them irritating'.

One group my husband and I led had a ground rule – negative speech was forbidden. We were not to speak negatively about someone; if there was a problem our concerns must be voiced in the other person's hearing. If someone started to criticize, the hearer was allowed to say, 'I'm sorry, I cannot listen to that until X is present'. So somehow we evolved a get-out clause! People would say, 'Dear old so-and-so, *bless him*...' and then we stuck the knife in! Bitterness cripples large parts of the church and keeps the bride in chains. If something happens to hurt us we get wounded. Bitterness is like dirt in that wound. Before I can be healed I have to choose to forgive the person who has wounded me. The Lord is longing to begin restoration but resentment locks him out.

Dr. David Yongghi Cho, Pastor of Yoido Full Gospel Church in South Korea, the world's biggest church, says that the greatest inhibiter of physical healing in Korea is lack of forgiveness. I remember once hearing Joy Dawson of Youth With A Mission speak about a time when she was asked to pray with a lady during a conference she was speaking at. Somehow she did not feel the power of God moving freely as she went to pray. She said to the lady, 'Let's just pray and see if either of us has done something to grieve the Lord.' As soon as she bowed her head she remembered a conversation she had had earlier with her husband in their room, in which she had spoken negatively about another Christian leader at that conference. The Lord instantly brought to mind the words in the Old Testament 'Do not touch my anointed ones'[83]. As soon as she had confessed and asked his forgiveness the sense of the Lord's power returned. This is a sobering story when we think of the amount of carping and criticism that is to be found in so many churches and even between church leaders.

This is an upside-down kingdom, blessing those who curse us, hurt us and ignore us. It is not fair, it cost Jesus the cross... how could it be easy? It costs us everything (including our sense of justice!) to forgive someone who has wronged us, but forgiveness is one of the greatest distinguishing characteristics of Christianity.

One day a student brought her friend to see me. I knew very little about the girl except that she found it difficult to meet my gaze. A sad story of abuse and betrayal came out as we talked together and she told me that as a young teenager she had endured panic attacks and felt so contaminated that she would sit behind parked cars in her road, hoping that one would run over her. The thought of ever forgiving the relative who had so harmed her was both outrageous and impossible to her. After some time, we asked the Lord Jesus to come and touch her. Her friend and I were about to witness a miracle! As we were praying we saw the girl's face begin to shine and beam, and suddenly her eyes flew open and she said 'WOW!'

She went on to ask if I had ever noticed she could never look me in the eye. 'That was because I always felt so dirty,' she said. As we were praying suddenly she saw quite clearly in her mind's eye the figure of Jesus coming towards her. He placed a white dress on her. 'For the first time I felt clean,' she exclaimed. What happened next, though, was the real miracle. Without any prompting, she began to pray for the man who had harmed her, forgiving him and asking God to bless him as he had just blessed her. As I listened to her passionate prayer, I learned a very important lesson – only those who know they are forgiven can forgive!

Much has been written about forgiveness, but the enemy has kept us largely ineffective as the bride of Christ. Even those outside the church can see how disunited we are, and often would rather choose secular friends who are less likely to speak behind their backs! We need to take a long, hard look at what forgiveness entails.

Forgiveness is not saying that the other person is right. It is saying that they may be wrong but I refuse to be their judge. It is not a one-off action. I remember once feeling very betrayed by the person I worked for. I had been reading a book about forgiveness and knelt down tearfully choosing to release him from my judgment. About a week later I was speaking about him to my mother and she said, 'Sounds like you need to choose to forgive him'. 'I did!' I exclaimed, outraged. 'It was a big deal. I found it really hard but I made the choice!' Right there I realized that forgiveness is releasing someone from judgment for as long as it takes. They may go on hurting us – God forgives us a hundred times a day. Forgiveness is a choice rather than an emotion, just as love for those we find difficult is often a choice first of all. I met someone who had been struggling all her Christian life because she could not feel forgiveness towards a woman who had harmed her many years before. When I asked her, 'Could you *choose* to forgive this person?' she said she could do that, and took her first steps to freedom immediately by speaking out her choice to release. Choosing over and over again to release someone from judgement will in the end bring a release in our emotions that is impossible to achieve by trying.

Forgiveness is not fair: it is letting the person go free in our judgement and thought life, and we would rather at least harbour a little resentment where no one can see it! But if we make the choice for freedom, we receive a host of gifts from the King's purse. Our prayers are free to be answered,[84] our thoughts are not dominated by bitterness, and a weight often rolls off our spirit that we didn't know was there until it is gone! Eventually, to move into all that God has for us in this area, we may need to get to the point of actively blessing the person we have found it hard to forgive! That truly is a heart set free.

As I read through the well-known passage in Ephesians 6 recently, I noticed a little phrase that I had not thought over: 'Stand then in his mighty strength'[85]. I began to ask myself what I understood by 'his mighty strength'. The film *Twister* is about a group of people who apparently suicidally chase after tornadoes in order to find a way of tracking them and providing an early warning system. There comes a moment when the tornado suddenly appears over the hill right in front of them and it is growling like a mighty wild beast. People looked rather sceptically at me when I said I liked that part! But that raw, untamed, majestic power sounded to me like the voice of God. The psalmist cries out, 'The voice of the Lord is powerful. The voice of the Lord is majestic. The voice of the Lord breaks the cedars...'[86] That is what you and I are to stand in – his mighty strength! The raw, untamed power that rules the universe! The word 'universe' means 'single spoken word', a word spoken by a power greater than any law governing the world we know. We stand against all that is thrown at us, 'for our struggle is not against flesh and blood, but against the rulers, against the powers, against the world forces of this darkness, against the spiritual forces of wickedness in the heavenly places'.[87] There have been times in my life when all I can do is to stand, there seems no strength left in me for battle, but I can (sometimes only just) remain upright.

A good general knows when to command the troops to stand their ground, and when to advance and take the field. In the chapter on wounding we have looked at some personal areas where we need to advance and reclaim areas long held captive. We go on the attack in our own lives as we take ground that the enemy has held for years in terms of fear, anger or a whole host of strongholds behind which he seeks to keeps us inactive and ineffective. We go on the attack in prayer for our family, for our friends, for our church, for our area and for our nation. If he can keep us inward-looking the enemy has won, for we will not prove much of a threat. He keeps us inward-looking when we do not want to move beyond the wounds to wholeness, but he equally keeps us inward-looking when we forget that church is a service station to arm and refresh us for the fight.

The media subtly and relentlessly vilifies Christians (and in particular those who are termed 'born agains'). TV programmes, documentaries and articles are often aimed at convincing the public that Christians are ineffective and futile or stop-at-nothing fanatics on a level with the Taliban, and the many-times inglorious history of the church furnishes plenty of examples for the media to draw on. The name of Jesus is spat out in derision, and is used a thousand times a day on the lips of those who do not know him, because the enemy wants to make it the most valueless word in the language. Our reaction to this is crucial in our day.

Perhaps now, more than in any other time in history we need to understand and live out the truth that the enemy is the devil and not people! His current strategy is brilliant and the church needs to be on its guard if we are not to play right into the hands of the opposing forces of Satan. Constantly subjecting the public at large to anti-Christian rhetoric is beginning to have its effect, but one object of this is to stir up God's people in anger and retaliation, to become exactly what they are being caricatured to be.

This is a day of all-out war, and God's people must be deeply centred in truth and the love of Christ, so that they recognize that the war is in the heavenly places. We can be so taken up with our little lives on the one hand, or the personal opposition on the other, that we can miss the call to rise up as an army of God, to become warriors in prayer rather than occasional pray-ers! The enemy may be twisting and manipulating but our fight is not against people, says Paul, it is 'against the rulers, against the powers, against the world forces of this darkness, against the spiritual forces of wickedness in the heavenly places'[88], and that war is won principally in the place of prayer. God's people may no longer make feeble excuses concerning why they do not pray... we pray to survive! We pray to rescue! We pray to take ground in people's lives and countries' regimes! 'He makes his angels... a flame of fire' (Hebrews 1:7)...how sure are we that when we pray mighty warriors are locked in combat? Are our prayers those which send angels to battle?

> *All heaven waits with baited breath*
> *For saints on earth to pray*
> *Majestic angels ready stand*
> *With swords of fiery blade*
> *Astounding power awaits a word*
> *From God's eternal throne*
> *But God awaits our prayer of faith*
> *That cries 'Your will be done!'*
>
> *Awake O church, arise and pray*
> *Complaining words discard*
> *The Spirit comes to fill your mouth*
> *With truth, His mighty sword*
> *Go place your feet on Satan's ground*
> *And there proclaim Christ's name*
> *In step with heaven's armies march*
> *To conquer and to reign!*[89]

Some of the early godly archbishops show us how to behave in a compromised society. Archbishop Alphege in the eleventh century was a deeply humble man who would not allow others to kneel before him but instantly also fell to his knees, that the glory went to the Lord he served. However, when it became necessary to stand for truth rather than compromise, Alphege paid the highest price rather than deny his faith. Archbishop Thomas à Becket refused to compromise the faith, and as his murderers entered Canterbury Cathedral the monks rushed to protect him. His last words were addressed to those monks, preparing for battle: 'Stop! We will not turn God's house into a fortress!' In other words, our place is not to barricade and defend, but to bless man, to praise God and to stand against the enemy in the evil day.

When I was young there was perhaps too much emphasis on end times, but it was a whole lot better than now when there is hardly any emphasis on them at all! Scripture tells us to read the signs of the times[90], and to live as though Jesus were about to come.[91]. As we read Matthew 24 with our present day in mind, we see signs of his coming.

Matthew 24:6 says there will be wars and rumours of wars. Terrorism in our day is a constant rumour of war. Nations will be rising, and there will be an increase in natural disasters. This is just 'the beginning of the birth pangs', says Jesus. He warns that his people will be in danger of falling away. We need to look carefully at the way we worship together when we emphasize not wrongly but too exclusively the place of experience or emotional satisfaction in our day. In digressing from scripture's emphases we can sow the wind and may reap the whirlwind.[92] What will happen to those who want just another touch from God, just another prophecy or good feeling, when persecution comes?[93]

People are leaving the church today in droves because, they say, it is tainted, imperfect, or irrelevant. They are right, of course: we are imperfect and will be until the day of Jesus Christ. The truth is that if the church were at war, as she is called to be, she would need to be spotlessly clean and holy because it is too dangerous not to be! Jesus is committed to her, in all her imperfections, but when she is not 'mission-shaped' and outward-looking she will die. The church as a bride, beautiful and deadly, is yet to be seen, but God is calling his people to war for the highest prize, to forever give up our pursuit of fool's gold.

The world monetary system could fall in a day – this has not been possible until recently. Stem cell research and cloning have potential for good but also for creating evil. Jesus says: 'As it was in the days of Noah',[94] so it will be when he returns. How was it in the days of Noah? Well, apart from sin and destruction, Genesis 6:4 says that there was direct intervention by the occult in the world we live in. Popular fantasy writers predict intervention in human affairs by fallen angels. And all this is before we speak about global warming, food shortages, the Aids epidemic, sexual deviation, and a compromised and divided church!

'Esther dear Queen, this is your day', said Mordecai at the darkest moment of Jewish history. 'You were born for this. Put on your crown and be seen, intervene and intercede now in new power, and if you perish you only do so in this world.' It is time to put down all our 'things' and to enlist in the battle. During the Second World War, people were not invited to join up. Nelson said famously,

'England *expects* that every man shall do his duty'. Like that Old Testament bride Queen Esther, we do not move until we are anointed, our skin saturated with the Spirit's holy anointing. This doesn't come from a day or a weekend set apart for God, it comes from a life consciously enlisted. Prayer is no longer something we feel we *should* do, it is something we have to do to survive!

Instead of reacting to the immediate, we need to strategize, to sit down with God and ask him for his strategy for our life. When did we last ask the Lord 'Where can I do most damage to your enemy?' University Christian Unions are coming under pressure to compromise their stance on purity or Lordship, laws are being passed whose interpretation could seriously threaten liberty of worship. We the bride must be revealed today in all the glory of holiness to which we have been called. We do not have a choice for much longer… we must become the shining bride he chose us to be, 'terrible as an army with banners'. Like the early church we are to rejoice when we are called upon to suffer shame for his name,[95] we seek his strategies in prayer and spend serious time crying out for movement in heavenly places, and we forgive and bless where we are derided or persecuted. As we do so, our Lord Jesus is able to cleanse his bride and reveal her in awesome splendour, his mighty power flowing unhindered through her as she becomes holy. The King's purse strings will be loosened and the true coinage of the kingdom will flow once more into his church.

True wealth is found in Jesus, and Jesus valued people – people snatched from the jaws of a devourer, from the darkness and captivity of death. That is true gold! There is nothing to compare with that kind of wealth! General Booth, founder of The Salvation Army, visited

Cecil Rhodes in Rhodesia, as it was then known. Rhodes was known for his love of gold and for exploiting both the miners and the natural resources of the country he lived in. He was fascinated by General Booth in whom he recognized a similar driving force, and he asked him one day what it was that motivated him. Without missing a beat the old man replied, 'To me, *men*, especially the worst, possess the attraction of gold mines!'

In every war there are reversals, pain and hardship, but our calling is to enlist thoughtfully and in sober understanding of the cost, knowing that victory is secure and speeds the day of betrothal for our King and his bride.

> *'Say not the struggle naught availeth,*
> *The labour and the wounds are vain,*
> *The enemy faints not, nor faileth,*
> *And as things have been they remain.*
>
> *If hopes were dupes, fears may be liars;*
> *It may be, in yon smoke conceal'd,*
> *Your comrades chase e'en now the fliers,*
> *And, but for you, possess the field.*
>
> *For while the tired waves, vainly breaking,*
> *Seem here no painful inch to gain,*
> *Far back, through creeks and inlets making,*
> *Comes silent, flooding in, the main.*
>
> *And not by eastern windows only,*
> *When daylight comes, comes in the light;*
> *In front the sun climbs slow, how slowly!*
> *But westward, look, the land is bright!*[96]

6

The Father is Seeking

True Worship

'Jesus said to her, "Woman, believe Me, an hour is coming when neither in this mountain nor in Jerusalem will you worship the Father. You worship what you do not know; we worship what we know, for salvation is from the Jews. But an hour is coming, and now is, when the true worshippers will worship the Father in spirit and truth; for such people the Father seeks to be His worshippers. God is spirit, and those who worship Him must worship in spirit and truth."'[97]

Diane[98] had suffered her father and mother's divorce some years before. Then her stepfather, a tempestuous man, walked out on them abruptly one day, taking with him many things that were of sentimental as well as actual value – including the car. She and her mother were Christians but were struggling with forgiveness and feeling understandably bitter. When we talked about praising

God in all circumstances she gave me an old fashioned look and said she understood the principle but doubted whether her mother would go for it!

To my surprise Di returned jubilantly after the Easter break, saying, 'Mum and I found it very hard to forgive or praise when we were so hurt and angry, but we sat down together and made a decision to release my stepfather from our judgment. Then we went on and thanked God for all he had done for us and even for the situation, because he is far greater. Imagine our surprise when we got home next day and found the car back in the drive, along with lots of the other things he had taken!'

Praise was perhaps the first Christian discipline that I learned in my Christian life and it was certainly the first discipline to slip! We are basically self-centred creatures, and praise and worship is giving worth or value to God just for who he is, no matter how we feel. This has become even more difficult in our postmodern culture. Of all the areas where we are tempted to go for fool's gold rather than true wealth, worship must be the greatest. We have often turned worship into a self-gratifying experience, and we will find that bad experiences can counteract good ones!

Turning to God our maker in thanksgiving and worship is a selfless act, yet because we were made for worship, this activity more than any other will unlock the King's purse and bring us gold. Far more importantly, it will lay gold at his feet, and glorify him. I remember praying with someone once and she said that as we had prayed she saw Jesus, with huge bulging sacks at his feet. He had reached down and slit one sack and thousands of gold coins spilled out. As she watched, he said, 'This is my treasure; the life of each one who comes to me is a coin in my treasury.' Love is a time-consuming choice. One of the most costly gifts in our modern lifestyle is time – it is the twenty-first century equivalent of the alabaster box of ointment that was tipped over Jesus' head by a woman who loved him.

Some years ago, Merlin Carothers wrote his book *Prison to Praise*[99] based on two scriptures: 'Rejoice ever more; pray without ceasing; in everything give thanks…'[100] and '…always giving thanks *for all things*'[101] (italics mine). He said, perfectly biblically, that we needed to give thanks in and for everything. This did not go down well with many church leaders who said, 'You cannot thank God for cancer, or other disasters, they are the work of the enemy'. That is true, but does it follow that we stop being thankful people as soon as something goes wrong? Is God sovereign? Is it not possible to ask him for healing yet to thank him in whatever state we find ourselves? We need to look closely at this subject, because in a day where the feel-good factor is paramount, we may turn to fool's gold all too easily. We think that true praise is singing songs, because they lift our spirits, when often our spirit lifts just because the music is exciting.

Why Praise?

First of all we do so because God is worthy. Worship is, of course, 'worth-ship' – giving God worth. My feelings or my present experience do not affect the fact that Jesus died on the cross for me or that God is mighty. In September 1991 my husband and I had to go to Guy's Hospital when the ultrasound found that there were some severe abnormalities in the baby I was carrying. This devastated us and we cried out to God on the way to the hospital for mercy, restating our trust in him in all circumstances. During the tests the radiographer was called away for about twenty minutes, leaving me up on the couch, and the young nurse with us turned to us and said, 'How is it you seem so peaceful at such a time?' We were honest about our pain, but talked to her about the goodness of God to us, and of Jesus and his love for her until the radiographer returned. Giving God worth at that time may have spoken to her, but it certainly lifted our spirits as we spoke out truth just when everything seemed blackest.

We praise also because God commands it. In his book *Reflections on the Psalms*, C.S. Lewis very helpfully addresses our anxiety that only a megalomaniac would demand worship!

> 'He is the Object to admire which (or, if you like, to appreciate which) is simply to be awake, to have entered the real world; not to appreciate which is to have lost the greatest experience, and in the end to have lost all... The miserable idea that God should in any sense need, or crave for, our worship like a vain woman wanting compliments, or a vain author presenting his new books to people who never heard of him, is answered by the words 'If I were hungry I would not tell you' (Psalm 50:12). Even if such an absurd Deity could be conceived, He would hardly come to us, the lowest of rational creatures, to gratify His appetite...'

'I had never noticed that all enjoyment

spontaneously overflows into praise unless (sometimes even if) shyness or fear of boring others is deliberately brought in to check it. The world rings with praise – lovers praising their mistresses, readers their favourite poet, walkers praising the countryside, players praising their favourite game – praise of weather, wines, dishes... I had not noticed how the humblest, and at the same time most balanced and capacious minds praised most, while the cranks, misfits and malcontents praised least... I had not noticed either that just as men spontaneously praise whatever they value, so they urge us to join them in praising it. "Isn't she lovely?" "Wasn't it glorious?" "Don't you think that magnificent?" The Psalmists in telling everyone to praise God are doing what all men do when they speak of what they care about.'[102]

God commands worship not because he is a tyrant but because praise completes our enjoyment of something. He commands praise because it is good for us, it realigns us and puts us in the place of faith, restored to his image. The Westminster Catechism says 'The chief end of man is to glorify God and to enjoy him forever.' If worship is what we were made for, then it stands to reason that we simply function best when our hearts are raised in praise.

When Di saw the dramatic results of praising God with her mother, she wanted to give a testimony on the Sunday. In the meeting was a young man who was rather incredulous. He and his family were similarly facing a hard predicament. His father had been made redundant and in the ensuing months had run up huge debts and had sunk into such depression that the rest of the family felt very anxious for him. The young man went home thinking 'This is idiotic. How can I thank God for everything when this situation is disastrous?' He looked up the scriptures and finally sank to his knees, saying, 'Well, it worked for that girl, so Lord I do choose to thank you for everything that has happened to my dad, and I choose to say you are wonderful in spite of everything that is happening now.' Two days later, he received a phone call from his mother to say that his dad had been re-employed by his old workplace, nine months after being laid off. They even offered him a more highly paid job than the one he had previously had, which helped to repay the debts he had incurred! Of course praise and worship are not penny-in-the slot actions, a sort of buttering up of the Almighty so that we can get what we want! However, as he take the choice to look at God and not at ourselves or the circumstances, faith in action frees the Holy Spirit to work in those very difficult situations.

We praise because it is logical. When I was younger my father often (rather smugly, I thought!) quoted Romans 8:28 to me when I was upset. 'All things ... work together for good to those who love God, to those who are called according to His purpose'. As I have gone on in the Christian life I realise what logic is in that verse. If you belong to a loving Father, *nothing* is a coincidence. He knew it would happen and he can and will bring good even out of the worst of circumstances. I recently met a remarkable couple in ministry whose dearly loved son committed suicide. Many in their town have been brought to consider Jesus, and some have found him, because of the continued faith and love of these people despite the tears and anguish. The wife said to me, 'Make no mistake, I want my son back. But as that is not going to happen, I thank God that he can use this terrible thing for his glory, and I long to bring him the fruit of all this pain'.

We praise God because praise is natural if we belong to him. Psalm 16 says, 'in your presence is fullness of joy' – you can tell the people who live in God's presence! Not because they are always happy. Happiness can be the result of temperament or circumstances; joy is independent of this. God is a happy God,[103] and we reflect his character as we give him praise. This is tough teaching but so essential, because it is the opposite of self-pity (or any other of the 'self' words). Many teach on prayer, fewer teach on praise, yet our whole life changes when we get hold of the principles of worship and praise.

What is Praise?

We give God worth by giving thanks – for what he has done. The list is endless, and as we start, more and more gratitude comes tumbling out. 'He made the heavens, he sent his son to die for me, he sent his Holy Spirit to empower me, he defeated the enemy at Calvary and in my life…'. We thank him for answered prayers, for food, clothes, shelter and far more. We start, we enter the gates with thanks,[104] because it gets our heart up and running. Many times the psalmist tells his soul to rise up – it would do us good to follow his example and speak to our own soul occasionally, 'Come on, soul, get up and stop this hand-wringing and declare the truth!' My soul can be sluggish and usually loves to wallow for a while in self-pity.

Catherine Marshall suggests[105] that we make three lists, one for the things we are thankful for, one for those we are less than thankful for, and the last list for things that we are downright unhappy about! After all, it is a command! As I start to make those lists perspective returns and I begin to chuckle at the more petty concerns that often keep me wallowing.

In the film *Spartacus* there is a famous scene where the tiny rebel slave army is seen arming for battle. They look pretty prepared, in fact, with what weapons they have to hand, and they are clearly passionate and resolute – you begin to hope against hope that somehow they might win the day. Then the camera pans back to the Roman army in perfect formation, spread out over the plain as far as the eye can see, and you quickly realize that the slave cause is lost before the battle even begins. A very similar situation occurs in 2 Chronicles 20 – one of my favourite chapters in the Bible. The people of God form a tiny band compared to the enormous army they are facing. They take their stand before God, with wives and children present, and King Jehoshaphat deliberately thanks him for who he is, and reminds him of his promises. Thanksgiving releases the prophetic, and the prophet Jehaziel rises to tell them, 'Do not be afraid or dismayed because of this great multitude, for the battle is not yours but God's... You will not need to fight in this battle. Position yourselves, stand still and see the salvation of the Lord, who is with you, O Judah and Jerusalem'.[106] The people rise to thank God and the priests fall down to worship: there are times of exuberance when we rise up to cry out our Lord's praises, and others when with awe and wonder we bow in silence and the enemy is miraculously defeated.

Once we have entered the gates with thanksgiving we go further into his courts with praise. On Jewish New Year, the people would sing Psalm 47 seven times! It is a Psalm of pure praise, not asking God for a single thing. When I was a young pastoral assistant I thought I'd try this out. We were doing a series on praise and I asked the midweek congregation to get into groups and just spend the time praising without asking for anything. We found it was practically impossible! Someone would start, 'We praise you dear Lord for this beautiful day… and we just want to pray for Beryl who cannot get out and about to enjoy it…' We discovered together that we were actually far more interested in God's hand than his face.

Types of Praise

We are all good at *spontaneous praise*, because, of course, we feel like it. Something happens to delight us and we cry out, 'Praise the Lord!' The Persian for the word 'praise' can be translated 'the bursting forth of a boiling heart'! When my husband was a student he walked through the countryside to his university full of the Spirit and of praise. He saw a field of cows and yelled out to them (very biblically!) 'Praise the Lord, all you cows!' They all obediently mooed, but whether with praise, amusement, or because they thought he was the farmer bringing food, we shall never know!

Then there is *sustained praise*. For me this is the hardest test of worship, because it is hard to praise God regularly and frequently regardless of feelings. After all, is this being dishonest? If we don't feel like it, should we do it? Sustained praise is when we choose to make Jesus king in our circumstances no matter what we feel. The psalmists are incredibly honest in telling God how they feel but they end by choosing to put their trust in him and praise him, deliberately recalling past benefits and affirming their faith in future grace.

How do we sustain praise? My own methods vary in my times with God. I give thanks, maybe listen to music, sing out worship songs or perhaps affirm my faith using scripture or the three lists Catherine Marshall suggests. When we feel too heavy to thank, we can speak our praise out loud or write a letter. Genuine feelings always follow the choice to worship. I used to keep a little notebook into which I put all sorts of things to aid me in praise: answers to prayer, verses of scripture or song, thanks for creation, art, music, nature, the human body, thanks for the facts of our faith, all the names and characteristics of God that I could think of! These lists help me to this day, when I am tired, worn down or low.

As a result of sustained praise the Holy Spirit is released in power. Jesus could 'do no mighty works' in Nazareth because of the people's unbelief. The reverse is also true. Praise is faith in action – we are declaring to God, the enemy and ourselves that our faith is in God, and this immediately releases the Lord to act!

There are three reasons why we don't sustain praise. First, we are simply not in the habit. We can start a joy-filled habit now, choosing to thank God for everything. We can play a game like Brother Lawrence at his kitchen sink, making worship an everyday part of life. Secondly, sustained praise costs us our self-pity. We just don't want to praise often, and prefer to enjoy our misery a little longer! Finally, the enemy hates praise! Remember that worship is what the war is all about. Lucifer coveted the worship due to God and he will do anything to stop us from turning our hearts to him. I once read an article about how a high-pitched dog-whistle can be inaudible to us but send animals crazy, and I often think that worship is like a dog-whistle to the enemy. Sometimes when someone has been involved with the occult they find worship almost impossible to sit through, until the Lord has freed them from the enemy's grip.

Hebrews 13:15 speaks of the *sacrifice of praise*. As a pastoral assistant in my early twenties I was asked to go to visit a housebound lady who had written to our minister requesting a visit. When I arrived at the door a quavering voice asked who it was, and a few moments later I was standing by the bedside of a tiny frail lady. She lay on a water bed with nurses coming in twice a day, as she was crippled with osteoarthritis and her bones broke very easily. Yet for me it was like entering heaven! This old lady's face shone with a light of fierce love as she spoke of her Lord. She said she could not help praising him for his wonderful love and grace to her, and she asked her nurses not to close her curtains at night so that she could look at the stars and remember his handiwork. One day I brought a tape recorder to play her Handel's Messiah. As the strains of the Hallelujah Chorus filled the room I thought that little saint would burst, so great was her luminous joy. She had so little in earthly terms to praise God for, but she had learned the secret of access to wealth beyond dreams.

It is a discipline to praise when everything is going wrong. Habakkuk exhorts us to rejoice even when everything around us is in turmoil: 'Though the fig tree should not blossom and there be no fruit on the vines, though the yield of the olive should fail and the fields produce no food, though the flock be cut off from the fold and there be no cattle in the stalls, yet will I exult in the Lord, I will rejoice in the God of my salvation'[107] (italics mine). Habakkuk is not exhorting us to be false and bubbly; sometimes we worship through tears and gritted teeth, but we are trusting him and as we do so he comes close to us. When Job was told of the death of all his children and the destruction of all he owned it says 'he fell to the ground and worshipped'. During a time of intense testing, Matt Redman wrote a well known song on this passage, with the decision ringing out: 'My heart will choose to say, "Lord blessed be your name"'. Jesus was 'a man of sorrows and acquainted with grief'[108] but he was also 'anointed... with the oil of joy above [his] fellows'[109] – why do you think children loved him? Zephaniah 3:17 says the Lord our God 'will exult over you with joy'. Apparently the word 'joy' here in the Hebrew can be literally translated as 'loud, animal-like shrieks'! God rejoices madly over us!

Worship is War

Worship is one of the chief weapons of the church. Not music, not noise (although worship obviously can include both) but the heart raising Jesus high. During one summer outreach we had been lent a coffee shop to run in the evenings and people dropped in for coffee and a chat. One night all was going well when suddenly a young girl could be heard screaming outside. Our young male students (who all seemed to be over six feet tall that year) raced round the corner to see if they could help, not thinking how aggressive this might seem to the man who was hitting her! He lashed out, breaking one student's nose and badly hurting another; the police arrived and suddenly the atmosphere in the coffee shop felt like that of a mortuary!

I gathered everyone together and we went out and said to the customers: 'We have decided to sing to you tonight'. As we began to worship, something happened which can only be described as a sense of light filling the place where we were. The customers seemed enthralled. Suddenly I saw that the guy who had been arrested had been released again and was standing outside the shop beating his head and fists on the boarding outside. As we continued to lift Jesus high, I saw my husband walk quietly up to him and put his hand on his shoulder. The young man spun round, grabbed his hand and burst into tears. We watched in awe as after a few minutes they sat on the pavement outside the shop, bowed their heads and began to pray.

The enemy fears and is often confused by worship. Years ago a friend told me about a meeting that she had attended where members of the local Satanist group had come to disrupt. As soon as the speaker rose they stood on their chairs and began chanting. Someone somewhere began to sing, another joined in, and soon the entire gathering were on their feet worshipping with all their might. When the time of praise died down, they found that the Satanists had left the meeting. The tiny Israelite army began to sing that his love endures forever: 'As they began to sing and praise, the Lord set ambushes against the sons of Ammon and Moab and Mount Seir…'[110]

To cap it all for Israel, there is a large prize at the end! They named the valley of victory 'Beracah', which means 'blessing', because without aggression on their part they are able to collect vast quantities of spoil. Sometimes the Lord amazingly changes the circumstances as we worship, sometimes he changes us. Either way, when we learn to praise and worship we receive far more of God's grace and mercy in our lives. This is because praise rids us of self so that there is simply more room for Jesus! One young schoolboy told me, 'It's like getting the sum, the answer and the prize as well!'

King's Purse – The Results for Us

One great result of a praising life is that we are less dominated by mood swings. A real sacrifice can be made when we surrender to God our moods and choose worship. If we only worship when we feel like it, we are like spiritual teenagers who are enslaved to our emotions. Worship, as faith in action, is declaring to God, to ourselves and to the enemy that despite how we are feeling, our hope is in a good God who gives good gifts to his people.

In John 8:44 Jesus calls Satan 'a liar and a murderer from the beginning'. Worship asserts truth in the teeth of the enemy's lies to us, as we assert God's sovereignty. We sing: 'It breaks a heavy yoke when you shout to the Lord'. Isaiah 10:27 talks of the enemy's yoke being broken 'because of fatness' (or 'because of the anointing'). In the days of Isaiah they would feed an ox with oil so that it grew strong enough to be able to burst off the yoke over its shoulders. As we worship God, his Spirit fills us with strength and we are able to burst off the heavy yoke of the evil one.

Another gift from the King's storehouse can be

enjoyed when we worship in this way, as we begin to know God! 2 Corinthians 3:18 says '...we all, with unveiled face, beholding as in a mirror the glory of the Lord, are being transformed into the same image from glory to glory'. You cannot keep gazing into your lover's face without becoming like him. Moses' face shone in God's presence. Arthur Blessit, a famous evangelist, had an encounter with Jesus one day that left his face shining so brightly that it terrified his wife so much that she shut the door on him![111]

The last thing that we hear King David say about himself is that he was 'the sweet psalmist of Israel'[112]. He could have described himself as a warrior, a shepherd, a king, but the most important thing he wanted, on his deathbed, was to be remembered as a worshipper.

Despite his many failings, David was a 'man after God's own heart' because he was a passionate worshipper.

> *'My enemy will say, 'I have overcome him,''*
> *And my adversaries will rejoice when I am shaken.*
> *But I have trusted in Your lovingkindness;*
> *My heart shall rejoice in Your salvation.*
> *I will sing to the Lord,*
> *Because He has dealt bountifully with me.'[113]*

Evangelism is natural when it comes from a thankful heart. When we took teams to evangelise on the streets, people might glance curiously at the dramas for a few moments, but the show-stopper was always worship. We were not singing to the crowd, we simply worshipped Jesus, and almost always there would be a crowd three deep all around us by the end of it. As people did not want to leave, we felt compelled to tell them why we were singing like this and still they didn't go! True heartfelt love for God, either on a personal level or corporately, is a very moving thing to see.

When I lived in London I became friendly with a Muslim girl and one day she said she would like to go with me to church. As we were worshipping at the end of the service, the person leading the service said, 'I think God is saying that if you want to, you will see him as you worship'. I was furious! 'How could someone say such a stupid thing on a day when I have someone from another faith with me?' I thought. I was certainly in no danger of seeing Jesus! Suddenly I became aware that my friend was sitting down weeping. 'Did you see him?' I gasped, too shocked for diplomacy. 'No,' she replied, 'But as people were worshipping, I felt him there.' As a result of this time of intimacy, we spent a long time talking about the God who comes close to his people.

Another gift from God's treasury when we worship is that intercession is natural. When we are praising, we come right into the heart of God and he gives us information through gifts of the spirit so that we can pray accurately. Billy Graham was asked if he had one last message for believers, what would it be? He replied 'Number one, PRAY; number two, PRAY; number three, PRAY.' Paul encourages us: ' Rejoice always; pray without ceasing; in everything give thanks; for this is God's will for you in Christ Jesus'.[114] If we did not worship as we interceded, the burden of God's heart would be too much to bear, but as it is, we lift our petitions, no matter how heavy they are, into the presence of the one who made the stars, and our faith rises as a result.

Self-centredness is defeated as we worship. My mother once visited a lady who was dying of cancer. She was on a heavy dosage of painkillers and said regretfully to my mother, 'I am no good at all to him now. My mind gets muddled, I can't even intercede any more'. My mother replied with great insight, 'You can love him. After all, that was what we were created to do, and most of us are just too busy to do what we were made for!'

Results of Praise for God

As we worship, the Lord's name is glorified and exalted. In the early church, believers met together to eat and to worship '…and the Lord was adding to their number day by day those who were being saved'[115]. People are drawn to Jesus as we worship. There is little doubt that churches are packed where genuinely worshipping people attract others to meet him.

It gives joy to God's heart when freedom comes to those he has created, and prisoners are released. The story of Paul and Silas in Acts 16:16–34 tells of literal physical release as they praised and worshipped God in a time of real adversity. Sometimes the release is in the spirit. Some years ago a newly converted friend of mine from a Muslim country was imprisoned with a number of fellow believers. After her release she wrote to me of her experiences, and I saw similarities with the account in Acts. She wrote:

> 'The Lord kept telling me "I shall be raised on the third day", so I knew a sort of rebirth needed to take place on the third day and was hoping

that I would be released. However, something even better happened. That day, blindfolded, I was taken upstairs to give my written statement and when I was in the room they unfolded my eyes and I saw the daylight out of the window. That moment, wonderfully, and incredibly the Spirit came inside me… For a few moments I couldn't stop my tears from running down, then I was filled with peace and joy and kept praying for the situation and for all the police… Even the initially hard-faced ones were very trusting, honest and friendly by the fifth day… the Lord was so good that the group who listened to our testimonies and took our statements were changed eventually, thus a totally new group of policemen took our statements…

When I was taken back downstairs to my room I was so filled with the Spirit that I danced and worshipped the Lord (very quietly)… I also saw a lovely shadow formed in the light coming under the bottom of the heavy metal door and it looked just like Jesus lying on his back. The shadow never left me afterwards. In moments of despair, being able to see Jesus' face was such an encouragement to me that I spent most of the rest of my time lying on my mattress, talking to the little Jesus under the door!'

Worship enables the people of God to push back the enemy. Some years back they used to have an attraction at some seaside resorts, where seats or large buckets were placed at the top and bottom of a cliffside, linked by a pulley. A volunteer would get in each bucket, and as one descended their weight would help the other to rise. John the Baptist said of Jesus, 'He must increase, but I must decrease'.[116] The higher we raise our Lord Jesus in worship, the more intimate we become with him, the lower the enemy and his lies, and guilt and fears sink beneath our feet. Hallelujah!

Every part of a surrendered life is worship, every time that we deny ourselves and choose forgiveness, grace and kindness, every time we serve others, or choose obedience to God's promptings instead of our own way, we are giving worth to the one we love. The apostle Paul writes:

> 'Therefore I urge you, brethren, by the mercies of God, to present your bodies a living and holy sacrifice, acceptable to God, which is your spiritual service of worship. And do not be conformed to this world, but be transformed by the renewing of your mind, so that you may prove what the will of God is, that which is good and acceptable and perfect.'[117]

Corporate Worship

In Argentina a few years ago the Spirit of God began to move in many churches and denominations. 'Before this time our services resembled a funeral service,' they said. 'We would have stirring music, someone would say something moving about the departed one, and we would all go home. But when the Spirit began to move, we encountered the presiding presence of God. He was the one who decided how things should be in our services after that!'

Much of scripture's teaching on the subject of worship is on corporate worship – starting with the morning stars who sang together at the beginning of creation. Throughout the Old and the New Testaments there is a sense that when the people of God come together corporately to the throne of God, joined by angels and saints, something very special happens. The astounding reality of our coming together on a Sunday is that God is enthroned on his people's praises.[118]. The church fathers called the Holy Spirit 'God's Kiss'. As we come close to him he comes intimately to us, either on our own or corporately. The reality of his presence is all we need or long for.

So many people are coming into church today with no previous experience of worship that we sometimes need to give practical guidelines so that they can just relax into relationship with a loving father. For example, between songs we can encourage the congregation not to look round, check the next song or the clock, or joke with someone else. We're in the presence of a King who comes close as we cry out to him. As we whisper out our prayers and adoration to him, we seek to be near him. Psalm 100:4 says that we enter his gates with thanks, moving up closer with pure praise. People may come in or out of the service, the worship band might (perish the thought) hit a wrong note – we are still reaching out to God. People are sometimes incredibly distracted by how short a time we have in the morning service, for example– but how long does it take to tell someone you love them and to hear their response? Encountering God is the whole point of our being here in worship, word and fellowship. The sermon may be perfectly structured, the music stirring, but if we do not encounter our King we have wasted the opportunity!

In the past I would often go home from church very frustrated if I did not feel the sermon or the music had lifted me into God's presence. One day I realized that while it is essential that these things are as good an offering to him as possible, my worshipping him did not depend at all on what was going on around me. It depended on God's worthiness to be praised! It sounds rather silly, looking back, but I had never before seen this clearly! The determination grew in me to encounter God *every* time I went to his house, and not to leave until I did. We go to God's house to join God's people or to receive helpful information to get us through the week, or receive fellowship and friendship, and all of those things are essential, yet we must still contend that the people of God primarily come together to *encounter God* together, to worship him and then as Ernest Southcott said, 'empowered by word and sacrament, to go out through the doors to be the church'.[119]

Oswald Chambers in his classic book *My Utmost for His Highest*, wrote, 'The secret of spiritual success is to be found in one word – ABANDONMENT'.[120] What does this mean for us in a postmodern culture? It is something we must seriously think about so that we do not end up choosing the pyrite of self-gratification but go for true worship. Jesus said, 'But an hour is coming, and now is, when the true worshippers will worship the Father in spirit and truth; for such people the father seeks to be his worshippers. God is spirit, and those who worship Him must worship in spirit and truth.'[121]

We are passionately to worship God with 'all our heart, soul, mind and strength'. Worship in our hard choices, in our work, and worship corporately, coming into his presence in awe, silence, exuberance and all the range of expressions that we see in scripture. Having said that I believe in places the bride has come to a dangerous place of polarization in our day, both extremes of which are not necessarily true worship.

Today we need to be seriously aware of using worship as a means of achieving an emotional 'high'. Music can, of course, be used this way in both secular and spiritual environments, and we are beginning to use secular methods of advertising worship music with worship heroes featured on the fronts of CD covers, and advertisements such as the one I saw recently which encouraged you to buy the worship CD to explore the depths of who you are! Who exactly are we worshipping at that moment?! Another promised worship for every mood – we have seriously lost the plot here! If we remember that from Genesis to Revelation the battle is for worship we can immediately see why there is such a determined effort on the part of the evil one to hijack worship in our day. Even times of soaking in his presence can become times for us to explore our feelings. This may be important and healing, as long as we do not confuse it with consciously and deliberately giving God worth.

There is a reason why we, the bride, need to be very clear about corporate acts of worship. Scripture teaches us that a day is coming when it will be difficult to worship God. The church's back will be to the wall (and indeed it is, in many places) and if we are raising a people who indulge in worship as a feel-good experience, what will happen to them in a day of persecution? However, a people who have learned to encounter Jesus and to stand in his presence regardless of temporary good or bad, will have wealth from a higher treasury and will have a rich source of replenishment in persecution.

Patrick Sukhdeo talks about visiting a group of Sudanese believers in a part of the country where the Christians were being massacred in large numbers. His little plane dropped him at night, and when he awoke in the morning he found that they had placed a mud cross on his hut. He saw other huts with mud crosses on them, and asked the believers why they had placed them there. The reply astonished him! 'When they come to kill us,' they said, 'we don't want them to mistake our Muslim neighbours for Christians and kill them by mistake, so we put crosses on our huts so they know who to kill!' Patrick said they were the most joyful people he had met, singing all day and praising God. He asked them why they were praising in such dire circumstances, and they said,

'Because he has given us another day to live.'

'Because he has saved us and loves us so dearly.'

'Because…' They kept finding more and more reasons to praise him! Surely this is true gold! My heart's desire is that we are raising a bride who will be able to stand in the evil day, with her head held high and the high praises of God on her lips, whatever befalls her.

Of course, this is only half the story. Folk in the opposite camp can sometimes equally struggle to get a biblical take on worship and feel that exuberance and emotion are not for God's house! We have only to look at the Old Testament and the example of David, to know that this is not the case. I remember coming home rather critical of something in church one day and the Lord challenging me. He seemed to be saying that actually he had enjoyed his people's heartfelt praises and I was the only one with a miserable carping spirit who missed the gold of what he was bringing! I was reminded of David's wife Michal, who criticized David's abandoned praise to his maker, and became barren as a result.[122] Barrenness spiritually always seems to come on the back of criticism and cynicism. We need to be very careful that we do not come against something that God has initiated.

In over thirty years of preaching, I have found that sermons on money or on worship are the most controversial topics in the Christian church. I suppose that is not surprising because both are subjects that can be about what we give worth to. The polarization today concerning corporate worship often comes between those who see the word as central and those who see the work of the Spirit as central to their services, yet there are many other nuances as well. Many evangelicals see communal worship as 'the singy bit' that has to be got over by employing what one church I went to called 'three bouncy choruses followed by three quiet ones'!

Today many are saying that worship leaders are the new evangelists. People are joining the church without any previous understanding of faith, and are learning their first words of truth through the songs that they sing. The Wesleys and The Salvation Army clearly used the same means to teach people truth. That does not mean we abandon teaching; it is more needed than ever in our day. It certainly means our songs and hymns must be based on truth and become a vertical expression of worship to God. Let us not get entrenched behind what makes us feel safe and comfortable, and above all let us not hurl abuse at those with whom we will be spending eternity – it is unlikely that as we enter heaven we will be asked for our musical preference!

> And He sat down opposite the treasury, and began observing how the people were putting money into the treasury; and many rich people were putting in large sums. A poor widow came and put in two small copper coins, which amount to a cent. Calling His disciples to Him, He said to them, 'Truly I say to you, this poor widow put in more than all the contributors to the treasury; for they all put in out of their surplus, but she, out of her poverty, put in all she owned, all she had to live on.'[123]

This passage encapsulates worship – giving the very best of everything we have and are to the one who gives all that he is and has, to us. We may have woken up like a bear with a sore head or have fallen out with the kids, our circumstances may be difficult, the question is will we lay it down for a short time in our week and reach out to the presiding presence of God?

I am by no means exhorting us to unreality here: we have looked at the 'sacrifice of praise' and seen that even when we are in a low place, turning to God in tears and trust can break heaviness, even when the pain remains acute. Here again we are looking at choosing to live in the wealth of the King's purse in times of hardship, rather than the choice of the fool's gold of our own sentimentality. God is our loving Father who can understand when we cry out and rail at him. Most of us would not be left standing if that were not the case! But when we choose the hard option of turning to him in worship, even in our pain, when we say with his agonizing Son, 'Not my will, but yours be done', we live as heirs of eternal provision, not as paupers who hurl abuse and live in squalor as a result.

'Who may ascend ... the hill of the Lord? ... He who has clean hands and a pure heart'[124]. When we come to God in corporate praise we are asking him to come right before our face. When he graciously responds and does that, the presence of his light is so powerful that we race for the altar to make our confession, taking our sins, our dreams, the business of everyday life – we take it all to his feet and leave it there.

In the Old Testament, Moses fearfully climbed the mountain to join an awesome God. Since the coming of Jesus, that same awesome God comes to us. The Hebrew word 'kabod' is translated 'glory' but it has the sense of great weight. Tommy Tenney tells a very moving story about a friend of his with a genetic disorder that made him so heavy that he broke people's furniture when he sat down. Weeping, he told Tommy how lonely this made him. He said that he would go to someone's house, and they would invite him in but he would stay with his hat and coat still on, looking around the front room to see if they had any furniture strong enough to hold him. Often he would make an excuse and return to his car in tears because there was just nothing strong enough to hold his weight. Tommy Tenney said that the Lord spoke to him at once. Tenney writes:

'How often does He stand at the back door of our assemblies with His glory still hidden by His "hat and coat" while He scans the room? We stop to count our spiritual goose bumps because we feel a cool breeze enter the room when the heavenly door opens. We tell one another, "Oh, God is here! He's visiting us again." Our singers rejoice and the band picks up the pace, but all too quickly it escapes us because we don't have what He is looking for…The answer is very simple. *We haven't built a mercy seat to hold the glory of God.* There is no place for Him to sit! We are happy to sit in our comfortable spiritual recliners all day, but the seat of God, the mercy seat, is a little different. It is the only seat on earth that can bear the weight of His glory and compel Him to *stay*… When He finds a house that has paid the price to build Him a resting place, He will come and He will stay.'[125]

It is only since the latter half of the twentieth century that Christians have felt the need to fit the worship service around us and our busy lives rather than fitting our busy lives around the worship service! (There is an extraordinary amount of stress engendered because the Sunday roast is waiting!) People's plans for the day have to be altered, because the service has made worship a priority. A gift of love cannot be forced or hurried.

The prevalent worldview is not appropriate for the house of God − we have not joined a club to fight for our rights or to expect decent servicing to gratify our personal set of needs. The only thing that needs to cause us anxiety is when we are not led sufficiently deeply into his presence to give him worth − however long it takes.

On one occasion when I was visiting Romania I

noticed that the presence of God always seemed to descend when one particular young man led the worship. I asked, 'How is it that you are so regularly anointed in this way?' and I shall never forget his reply. He said, 'I don't want everything to be a surprise when I get to heaven. I want to say, "Yes! I know this. I was living in it already on earth."'

Corporate worship was the cause of war in heaven. The enemy Satan longed, and still longs, for the worship due to God – it is the most contested activity we will ever undertake! Notice how the worship group so often comes under attack – this is only a disaster when it is the people of God doing the attacking! We should expect a reaction if we are being used to bring the presence of God closer to his people. We can become distracted by people around us, by musicians or singers. When I am distracted, I often close my eyes and reach out to God who is here, telling him I are not going until I have encountered him! Then, like King Jehoshaphat in 2 Chronicles 20, we discover that worship sees off the enemy.

Worship is a love relationship. Moses cried out to God to accompany his people: 'Is it not by Your going with us … that we, I and Your people, may be distinguished from all the other people who are upon the face of the earth?'[126] Moses says God's presence is the distinguishing characteristic of God's people. David, in Psalm 22, goes on to say that worship means that God comes close, seated on our praises. We often regard worship as somewhat like a 'chick flick' – a bit soppy and sentimental, but it is unlikely that this is what we will encounter in heaven. Having said that, we do need to realize at some point that love just isn't cool! Some of us may never have been mushy in public, but others of us remember doing things we vowed we would never do in public, like gazing into each other's eyes. Love truly frees us from the tyranny of self, and that is what happens in worship.

I remember a mature student who had a pretty tough and sinful life before he found the Lord. Normally 'Mr Cool', this young man would try never to miss the worship. I would see him sometimes run in at the back when he was late for the start of the meeting. He would drop his backpack and reach out his arms to God in what looked like a sigh of relief. Other members of that group would dance before the Lord sometimes. A visitor might think 'What a lot of emotional froth!' but only my husband and I knew that so often those joyful dancers were the girls from abusive backgrounds, whom Jesus had healed. They loved him fervently and visibly.

In the old marriage service couples vowed to one another 'With my body I thee worship'. We are the body of Christ here on earth, and our function is to worship. Gerald Coates said, when asked why he danced before the Lord, 'Because I can't fly!' Dancing or expressing yourself exuberantly might not be your style, and God wants us to express our worship in a way that is appropriate to our personality. We simply need to ask him to free us from consciousness of self and bring us before an awesome throne when we come to worship corporately.

More importantly, worship should be a lifestyle. Just as a marriage will founder if it has sporadic expressions of love followed by neglect the rest of the time, so it is with worship. If we have not encountered God in worship all week, no wonder we are volatile when we meet together! We may be 'high' when there is a great band and we feel fine, but we're downright depressed when it's one guy and a guitar! Are we confident that we are joined by angels with a similar purpose, to worship? When we make praise and thanksgiving a habit, the Holy Spirit is released into daily situations, and our corporate worship becomes a powerful paean of praise. The Lord will not be standing at the door looking in, then, but able to take his throne in the midst of his people; and his presiding presence will rule, rather than our own little agendas.

When our confidence is in the Lord and not in the size of our congregation or the expertise of our musicians, people are immediately attracted to Jesus. In one congregation we tussled with the prevailing thought that in order to be user-friendly we ought not to have worship for evangelistic services. We decided that although worship might be unfamiliar for people, we needed to explain simply and clearly why we worshipped and then just get on with it. As Moses said, the thing that distinguishes us from the rest of the world is the palpable sense of God with us! To our surprise and delight, most of the people who came commented positively on the worship. They said that they spent their time looking at people's faces (sometimes wondering 'what they were on'!) and that it seemed clear to them that they had a relationship with an unseen but real friend. Often they came back voluntarily because they wanted to be with a worshipping people again. Others dated their conversion from a time in the worship when God came close and spoke directly to them. When God comes close to us we hear his voice; after all, you tell your friends your secrets. When we sense his presence close, it is good sometimes to stop singing and listen as he so often speaks with words of knowledge in worship.

Not only do we hear his voice in worship, but we feel

his touch. We took a number of people to a large worship service in London on one occasion. None of them had ever experienced anything like it and we were all aware of God's intimate presence that night. Two of our number were overwhelmed by the Holy Spirit and received new gifts from him without anything having been said during the worship. One guy looked somewhat odd. He seemed to me, as I opened my eyes, to be doing his exercises: bending down and touching his toes! He explained afterwards that he had put his back out for some weeks and during the worship he felt God heal him; he was checking out all the things he could not do before!

Sometimes we dread corporate worship just because we *do* feel God's touch there. A church leader sorrowfully said to me, 'People so often stop coming to church at sad times, because they are afraid of the tears being released, yet this is in fact the safest place for that to happen!'

Even if we do not hear or feel anything when we come to worship, we have the privilege of being in the presence of an awesome king. Let us be like Obed-edom in the Old Testament, who kept the ark of the covenant after David was offended by God's rebuke.[127] Obed-edom and his household were so blessed in the presence being with them, that when David came to bring the ark to Jerusalem, Obed-edom could not bear to be parted from it and later he is listed as a doorkeeper in the house of God. He was so desperate not to be parted from the tangible presence of God, that he went with it wherever it went. Like the psalmist he would have said, 'I would rather be a doorkeeper in the house of my God than to dwell in the tents of wickedness'.[128]

We are coming in worship before an awesome throne,

joined by myriads of angels, joined by friends, relatives and saints throughout the ages who are already worshipping in heaven. We are in the presence of Jesus, our King, our brother, our master, our friend, our shepherd. He is robed in white, says John in Revelation, with eyes of fire, which nevertheless meet ours in love. His feet are like burnished bronze, standing in triumph upon every anxiety or pain we face today. Let us come together to worship him. 'With gold of obedience and incense of lowliness, these are the offerings to lay on his shrine.'[129]

> *'Love bade me welcome: yet my soul drew back,*
> *Guilty of dust and sin.*
> *But quick-eyed Love, observing me grow slack*
> *From my first entrance in,*
> *Drew nearer to me, sweetly questioning*
> *if I lacked anything.*
>
> *"A guest, I answer'd, worthy to be here":*
> *Love said, "You shall be he."*
> *"I, the unkind, ungrateful? Ah, my dear,*
> *I cannot look on thee."*
> *Love took my hand and smiling did reply,*
> *"Who made the eyes but I?"*
>
> *"Truth, Lord but I have marr'd them: Let my shame*
> *Go where it doth deserve."*
> *"And know you not, says Love, who bore the blame?"*
> *"My dear, then I will serve."*
> *"You must sit down," says Love, "and taste my meat."*
> *So I did sit and eat.'*[130]

7

Dividing Your Bread with the Hungry

Gold Given Away

'Is this not the fast which I choose,
To loosen the bonds of wickedness,
To undo the bands of the yoke,
And to let the oppressed go free
And break every yoke?

'Is it not to divide your bread with the hungry
And bring the homeless poor into the house;
When you see the naked, to cover him;
And not to hide yourself from your own flesh?

'Then *your* light will break out like the dawn,
And *your* recovery will speedily spring forth;
And *your* righteousness will go before you;
The glory of the Lord will be your rear guard.

'Then *you* will call, and the Lord will answer;
You will cry, and He will say, "Here I am"
If you remove the yoke from your midst,

The pointing of the finger and speaking
    wickedness,
And if you give yourself to the hungry
And satisfy the desire of the afflicted,
Then your light will rise in darkness
And your gloom will become like midday.

'And the Lord will continually guide you,
And satisfy your desire in scorched places,
And give strength to your bones;
And you will be like a watered garden,
And like a spring of water whose waters do not fail.

'Those from among you will rebuild the
    ancient ruins;
You will raise up the age-old foundations;
And you will be called the repairer of the
    breach,
The restorer of the streets in which to dwell.'[131]

The italics in the above passage emphasize where the hidden wealth of the King's purse may be found. Isaiah 58 tells us that the more we give away of ourselves, our love, our time, our resources, the greater will be our ultimate wealth. To the western world this seems like the ramblings of delirium! We know in theory that this is God's purpose, but we are often locked into a lifestyle that makes giving an impossibility, apart from donating a dollop of cash from time to time.

A Non-Fictional Parable

Recently a few of us have been involved in setting up a congregation on a nearby housing estate. One night one of our members had a dream...

Peter had gone to bed worrying about his marketing budget at work. In his dream the Lord came to him and said, 'Peter, what do you want?' He replied, 'Lord, I want half a million pounds for our marketing budget!' The Lord said, 'No, Peter, what do you really want?' Not getting the hint, Peter replied, 'Lord, I really want half a million pounds for our marketing budget!'

The Lord said to him, 'What is more important to you, what is going on in the church, or your work?' Without hesitation he replied, 'The church'. He then found himself praying in an uncharacteristic way for plumbers to pipe the love of God into the community, for electricians to bring light to dark places, for bulldozers to take down the walls of division, for drainage consultants to clear away the slurry of the devil's lies, and for us to fearlessly go where the needs are greatest.

When he had finished, the Lord said, 'Now, Peter, what else do you want?' He replied, 'Lord I really do need half a million pounds for that marketing budget'. The Lord replied, 'Look in the Yellow Pages!'

Peter woke up the next morning chuckling at the absurdity of the last part of his dream. After all, who ever finds £500,000 in the Yellow Pages? When he went downstairs, a copy of the Yellow Pages was lying open on the table and he glanced casually at it, seeing an advertisement from one of his firm's competitors. How ridiculous, he thought. 'We never get anything from this type of advertising.' On a whim he rang a colleague to ask if their firm advertised in the Yellow Pages, and if so, how much they spent? The reply came back, 'Yes, we do advertise there and elsewhere nationally, and we don't get any work from advertisements.' Peter immediately stopped all unproductive advertisements and was in receipt of more than his request!

I was in the middle of writing about whether we are seeking the King's purse or fool's gold when this event occurred, and it seemed like a perfect parable to identify true wealth. We are so caught up with the immediate that so much of the time we fail to see God's wider, deeper vision for our lives and – far more importantly – for our world. We see difficulties, waiting, deserts, wounding and suffering as hindrances to our valuable lives. God sees these things as the chisel that chips away the precious from the worthless, the fire that melts away the dross and leaves pure metal. In his inexorable love, the shepherd takes us through dark valleys to places where true treasure may be found. Sometimes it is etched painfully into our lives, that the face of our Lord may be reflected to those who are impoverished in ways we will never experience.

Yet because he loves us, the temporal things are also covered by the King. He may bring us to a place of prioritizing afresh, we may find the things we once thought were important have evaporated like dew in sunlight, but if we seek his kingdom first we find all these things are added to us!

Do you dream? Lawrence of Arabia's words are true: 'Those dreamers of the day are dangerous men for they may act upon their dream with open eyes and make it happen'. On 'Giving Sunday' in churches, we often have the parable of the talents as a reading, where more was given to the ones who invested their small amount, but everything was taken from the one who hid his money in the ground. But this passage was not uttered by Jesus to induce guilt on 'Giving Sundays'! This is a call to wisely invest our entire lives: our love, our time and our sacrifice, and yes, our money too, in the kingdom of God.

Do you dare to ask God for visions? I was speaking to a Ladies' conference one day and asked them if God had put any dreams inside them. One elderly lady told me that she visited the elderly and dying because it was the most important time in their life and they needed someone to sit with them, to love them and to tell them of the hope there was in Christ. Her dream was to raise a team of older people to come with her. Another well dressed lady told me of the vandalism which was a by-product of frustration in the youth on her estate. I thought she was about to complain about them but instead she said, 'My dream is to set up a pub without beer for these young people. Somewhere they can hang out and feel proud of.' We may feel terrified or challenged by the great visions, such as Reinhart Bonke's cry 'Africa for Jesus!' but we can start right where we are. Every one of us can do something. Our Father is a creator and some of his creative Spirit has spilled into every one of us. Most of us live far beyond our means today. We become bankrupt emotionally, and borrow resources we cannot renew in terms of our work, our family commitments and our spirit. Stop for just a moment and ask yourself these two questions. First, 'If I didn't have the demands on my life that I do now, what could I invest myself in?' Secondly, 'Lord, is there any way I could start to fulfil that even now?'

It may sound strange, but sometimes people do not find a dream or vision for their life because they are waiting for something as yet undiscovered to appear! I used to be disappointed, when I was younger, that I was blood group O. I would have liked to be a more interesting and useful grouping, if I were donating my life's blood! That was until a sensible nurse pointed out that if blood group O was the most usual blood group, it was also in most demand! There is so much need that whatever our gifts and desires, they can be matched with the world's need and change it significantly.

If your dreams are of personal glory they will be refined if you go on with God. They may be fulfilled if you are practical as well as ambitious, or they will fall to the ground. If you dream of *God's* glory, the path to fulfilment will be the way of the cross. It will include pain, setbacks and heartache, but the fruit will last forever. Today so few men and women or young people actually dream for God! If the enemy cannot stop us dreaming he will try to sidetrack us. I used to say to our students when they were preparing to leave us, 'Let's take the general's position a moment'. In times gone by, a general would observe the lie of the land from the top of the nearest hill. His concerns were to see where the enemy was weak, and where he was strong. The enemy was watching them and wanted to know where they were weak. It is the wise dreamer who knows himself and plans carefully, so that not only will their dreams come to fruition but they will not be spoiled by the craft of the enemy. The converse is also true: we can observe where the enemy is weakest in our lives and consolidate the ground.

Considering the pressure and peril of this darkness,

dare we face God *without* both a dream and a plan for executing it? 'Give up your small ambitions,' said missionary Francis Xavier. Generally it is the tyranny of the urgent that stops us from executing long-term goals to change our world and gain wealth from the King's purse. There are opportunities everywhere we look and as we submit to our local church leadership and seek wise counsel, there is no reason why we should not be world-changers. We will make mistakes – but this is not a problem if we stay in a strong, secure relationship of accountability within the family of God.

In Isaiah 54:2, the Lord speaks through the prophet, saying, 'Enlarge the place of your tent; stretch out the curtains of your dwellings…'. A tent is very vulnerable until it is at full stretch, but at that point it can withstand storms. At that point it can withstand storms. God designed us to be at full stretch spiritually. David says, 'I shall run the way of your commandments, for You will enlarge [stretch] my heart'[133]. We need to ask God to stretch our hearts! If the evangelical church would only stop praying for revival and start praying for and ministering in the heart of God, do we not think revival would come? It would be a revival, moreover, that would lead to transformation in society and not just within the walls of the church. Jackie Pullinger speaks of our having 'hard hearts and soft feet', where we need to be praying for soft hearts and hard feet to run to those in need.

This subject, above all, calls us to leave the pursuit of fool's gold and to seek to give, sometimes to give out of what appears to be an empty barrel, and to find wealth poured in from an inexhaustible supply. Condemnation often comes when we start to look at need: there is so much need everywhere we look that often we are overwhelmed. As we look closer at this vital subject we need to ask the Lord to impress upon us what he has for us to do. No one can do everything, but everyone can do something.

There is a very clear link between revival and justice issues in scripture and down through history. It was Christians who led the anti-slavery lobby, some say this came on the back of Wesley and Whitfield's preaching, others say that dealing with justice issues was the catalyst to revival. Isaiah 58 says if we make our sacrifice by reaching out to the poor and needy, our own light will shine. Those of us who are taking discipleship seriously are struggling to find a way to serve God and live a peace-filled life. How can I possibly have meaningful time with God, give adequate attention to my work, spend quality time with my family *and* become involved with justice issues, or even care for one other person effectively? We all have different rhythms of life. I am often frustrated that others achieve so much more than I do in the time given, but I must seek God's heart for his world, because that is what is most important to him, and if I long to do so and struggle and pray to that end, God will 'supply all my needs according to his riches...'

Some years ago Kurdish refugees were massing in their thousands on the Iran/Iraq border. Their suffering was acute and aid agencies were hurrying to the scene. A TV crew were intrigued by a Jew from Haifa who was present with a vanload of bottled water for the refugees. It was an unusual sight to see a Jew helping Muslims, and as they interviewed him the man told them that he was sitting at home in comfort in Haifa and had switched on the television only to be confronted by the plight of the refugees. He thought, 'I can fly out and buy bottled water and take that to them! Anyone can do that!' Anyone can. Cameron Townsend said, 'If we will do the possible, God will do the impossible.'

Jesus tells an enquiring lawyer[134] that the most important things for us to do are to love God with all our heart, soul, mind and strength, and our neighbour as ourselves. Trying to wriggle out of the discomfort, the lawyer (no doubt with a typically Semitic shrug of the shoulders) replies, 'Who is my neighbour?', and he is answered in an indirect fashion with the parable of the Good Samaritan. What, in fact, is the answer to his question? Jesus is surely saying, 'The one who needs me is the one who is my neighbour'.

'Let the oppressed go free.' Jesus echoes these words from Isaiah 58 in his manifesto when he says he has come to set captives free. I have friends who are in prison today, longing for a touch with the outside world, for someone to care that they exist. We do not need special skills to write to them, sit with them or to love them. Chuck Colson, the founder of Prison Christian Fellowship, tells of a lady in her nineties named Myrtie Howell[135]. Myrtie had endured a hard and pain-filled life and finally seemed set to end her days sadly in the miserable high-rise apartment block for old people in which she found herself. She said to the Lord, 'I would like to die now, please,' and the Lord replied with three words which I would never have used to a depressed old lady! He said, 'Write to prisoners'.

Myrtie Howell was not particularly literate, and did not know how to start, so she just wrote a letter saying that she was a grandmother who loved and cared for them and would be prepared to write to anyone who needed a friend, and she posted it off to the nearest prison. The chaplain sent her ten names and she began corresponding with people who had no one else to care for them. By the time that Chuck Colson visited her, she was surrounded by Bibles and commentaries, caring for prisoners, praying for them, writing to them and answering their questions. She was writing to up to forty prisoners a week across the country! We cannot say that there is nothing we can do! We are never too busy, too young, too old, too infirm, too incapacitated to show the love of God to one person. I received a letter yesterday from someone in prison who had discovered the treasure of the King's purse. He wrote: 'When I finally leave prison, I will carry with me an invisible satchel full of gold refined by years of fire. No one could steal it. And even if they could it would be useless to them. It's my training for my future mission on earth and ultimately for my eternal mission; to be the bride of Jesus Christ.'

However, there are plenty of other prisoners: captives of unworkable situations. Debt, for example, is one of the greatest social problems in the West, according to sociologists. When God's people begin to get involved in social action, with the love of Jesus, society begins to change.

Some churches offer supervised access visits to couples going through divorce. I remember one girl telling me of a neighbour who used to take her in as a teenager. The girl had a family, but was never shown love, and this woman simply taught her to cook and sew, doing all the things that a mum would do. I do not know you or your busy day, but I do know that if we are too busy to stop and show the love of God to one individual on a regular basis, we are too busy. The strange thing is that if we do not 'divide our bread with the hungry', we ourselves become impoverished as a result. We have no lasting wealth in the bank of our soul.

I heard someone tell the story of an American GI walking up the street in London at the end of the Second World War. His eyes were drawn to a small boy who was gazing longingly at some steaming fresh buns placed in a bakery window. The GI entered the shop, bought a bag full of buns and gave them to the little boy. The boy looked up at him in amazement and said, 'Mister, are you God?' When we learn to give and to be generous, the world looks on and says, 'Is that God?' I found early in my Christian life that if I tried to browbeat people with the gospel, they didn't want to know, but when they were going through a tough time and I turned up on their doorstep with a meal or a cake, *they* would talk to *me* about God. Funny, that!

One year, we took a team of students on a mission to a town in Somerset. The young people were doing various evangelistic activities, but we discovered that the local playground was littered with broken bottles, hypodermic syringes and all sorts of things that could harm the toddlers who used it. One afternoon the whole team went up to the playground with black sacks to clean it up. A couple of young mothers walked past and asked what we were doing, and when we told them they said, 'But it will just be full of those things again by next week!' We agreed that this was so, but for this week, it would be a safe environment for their children. The ladies left us shaking their heads and we felt rather foolish. Ten minutes later they were back, having arranged childcare for their toddlers, and brandishing brooms and brushes. As they set to work to help us, they asked, 'Why are you doing this for us?' We were able to talk to them of a God who cares about them: about the society they live in, as well as for their souls. The gospel is not just about personal piety, it is about lifestyle. Clive Calver (then the head of the Evangelical Alliance) was called up by the BBC when they were allocating more air time for religion. They said that the Buddhists had asked more time to teach Buddhism, the Hindus to teach on Hinduism and the Muslims had asked for more time for Islamic instruction. Clive said, 'I want to talk about education, I want to talk about health, I want to talk about unemployment, because these are the issues on the heart of God!'

Hebrews 6:1 speaks of 'repentance from dead works'. Dead works are not necessarily unspiritual activities, they are simply the things we undertake that have not been initiated by the Spirit of God. We frequently need to ask ourselves the question 'What is God saying "Yes" to for me?' I have endless energy and vision for that! I find that when I work with needy people, things surface in me that I don't like very much. Of course needy people can be manipulative and demanding, and we need to know how to deal wisely with that. However, my heart's reactions are so often sinful! When we lived in our previous home there came a time when it seemed to me that all the tramps in that city found out where I lived and would turn up to ask for sandwiches and something to drink. I was happy to give them something, but then they started to turn picky! They would say, 'Haven't you got any other sandwiches today? Can I have coffee, not orange juice?', and I started getting upset. I said one day, 'Lord, this is no use! They will never change, I am just being a doormat!' I felt him gently reply, 'Are you loving them, or just your agenda for them, then?'

One young teacher in her first job came to a Bible study one night in floods of tears. She said, 'It's so hard to discipline a child who is disrupting the class, when you know the pain they are going through and you don't want to add to their rejection!' She told us of a little six-year-old who would come into the classroom, pull her little knickers down, look in the mirror and cry. Getting angry doesn't help – abuse is often the product of being abused, a vicious circle that seems unbreakable, but we can help to heal. These problems are all about us and the truth is most of us are compassion-fatigued, or simply outraged. It is easier to give money, but we must *be* the gospel – the good news – to our society.

'Divide your bread with the hungry'.[136] Look at Hannah's song, the Magnificat, and many of the psalms – the constant reiteration of God's heart for the poor. The Pentecostal revival was among the poor, and to this day revival often comes where people have nothing apart from God – he loves to reach the lowest. The story is told of two young men in the nineteenth century, who were walking down a road in the east end of London, observing the deprivation, violence and poverty, wrought in the main by gin. One of the young men turned to the other, a medical student, and said, 'You take the children, I'll take the adults, and together we'll change the world'. His name was William Booth and he founded The Salvation Army. It changed the destinies of thousands of people around the world as it fed their bodies as well as their souls and gave hope where there was despair. The young medical student to whom he spoke was called Thomas Barnardo, and his name is synonymous with the rescue of children from his day and right up to the present time. World-changing is possible! Every one of us can change the world we live in, every one of us must do so.

Are the poor always those without money, or the homeless those without a house? There are many well-dressed people in our society who have no one to care whether they live or die. Some years ago I had a friend who had a part-time cleaning job. She wanted to go on holiday but was afraid of losing her job so I offered to do it for a week while she was away. When she returned I asked her about one place I had cleaned. It was very neat and well-ordered and belonged to a businessman, but the unusual thing I had noticed was that there was one unsigned birthday card sitting on the top of his TV. 'Yes,' replied my friend. 'The sad thing is that it sits there all year, and on one day each year, the card changes. He obviously sends it to himself.' Loneliness freezes people solid. It is one of the worst evils in our society and has reached epidemic proportions. In *The Lion, the Witch and the Wardrobe*, Aslan, once resurrected, enters the witch's domain and confronts those she has turned to stone. He breathes on the statues and a thin line of colour appears, quickly spreading outwards as they come into life and colour.[137] Love does that.

Removing rejection. In Luke 4:18, Jesus said that he had come to bring 'recovery of sight'. This did not just refer to physical sight. When Jesus healed the sick, sighted people saw there was a God of power and love. It is time to dream some dreams!

When my husband and I were younger we talked endlessly about how to reach those who never darkened a church door. We decided that we should ask him to send us a shop, but the only problem was that we had no money at all to put towards buying it! We decided to pray together every day for three months and see if God confirmed the idea. As we had no money we said, 'Lord, if this is something you want us to pursue, please send us a large amount (we had thought of £5,000), as a small financial gift would not be enough to put down on the lease of a shop'. We also asked him to speak to us by confirming this vision through the scripture. Towards the end of the three months three things happened in quick succession. The first was that my husband was given a £2,000 rise in salary, completely unexpectedly. The next day we opened a Christmas card and out fell a cheque from his uncle with a simple note: 'I was going to leave this to you when I died but I have decided to give it to you now'. The cheque was for £3,000! The third thing to happen was that same day someone gave us a scripture – it was Malachi 3:10: '"Bring the whole tithe into the storehouse, so that there may be food in My house, and test Me now in this," says the Lord of hosts, "if I will not open for you the windows of heaven and pour out for you a blessing until it overflows"'. We bought a coffee shop and people came to us who had been rejected in terrible ways, people who had been victims – God met them in an unthreatening environment and began to work in their lives.

Sometimes the church itself has become a pointing finger of rejection – 'Clean up your act!' 'God hates divorce!' 'God hates homosexuality!' God *does* hate these things, but he doesn't hate the people of course! We need to understand the philosophy of our day, we're lazy. If we want God's heart for our generation, we need to work at it, to know how postmodernism, 'new age' and pluralism affect our society, to know our Bible so we know truth rather than just give when there is an emotional response.

'*Satisfy the desires of the afflicted.*' Do you doubt that we need to be full of the Holy Spirit? We must overflow with praise and song and laughter, or the darkness would destroy us. We need the joy of Jesus if we are to maintain our way and go to those in need and pain, in poverty and misery.

Isaiah 58:8 says that you will not get left out! God's order is brilliantly illustrated in 1 Kings 17 where that outrageous prophet, Elijah, is sent by God to meet a widow. She is about to use the last of her flour and oil to make a final simple meal for herself and her son, before preparing to die during the famine. The prophet asks her to make the meal for him first, and amazingly, she does! As a result of her faith-filled generosity, the flour and oil never run out until the end of famine in that place. We often feel, 'I'd love to get God's heart for the world but I need to sort myself out first'. Bake that cake for him first: it's a scriptural principle that opens the King's purse most effectively. Then you will be sustained. The promise is that if we do not pursue the fool's gold which simply buys us temporary comfort, but if we give to those in need, we will be refreshed, watered, irrigated in our spirit, and the society where we live will begin to change significantly.

But we cannot leave it there. What about God's heart for the nations?

In the 1980s, the radical Christian singer Keith Green made himself unpopular in some quarters by saying that you had to obey the last order of a commanding officer in the army until another is given. Since Jesus' last command to us was 'Go into all the world', he reasoned that we had to be called to stay! And if we were called to stay, he continued, we have only one option – we must take responsibility for sending someone else! I have sent scores of young (and not so young) people into the mission field, and some stay, but they get discouraged and exhausted. You may be the means of someone staying – by loving, by writing, visiting, or financially supporting them.

If you are a parent, take one moment to imagine what it would feel like to watch your child die in front of your face – of hunger or hunger-related diseases – and be unable to do anything. 42,000 children die in this way each day. In Russia and many other countries of the world, there are hundreds of thousands of street children taking cover from the bitter winter under the manhole covers in the streets, starving, or burning themselves to death on the pipes underground. What are we doing about it? Can we do something? We can start by praying. In Psalm 2:8 the psalmist exhorts us to ask for 'the nations as your inheritance'. If our Lord Jesus will not return until the inhabited earth has heard the gospel, we must get into all the inhabited earth! It is so possible in our day. It takes the people of God to take the call seriously. To pursue the wealth that is found in giving instead of hoarding.

First of all we must *ask*. Ask for God's heart. Ask for a nation to pray for. Maybe you come from there, or you have friends in that country or support a missionary there. If that is not the case, ask God to put a country on your heart. Seek information about the population, religions, people groups, and needs of that country – its physical, social, political, and spiritual needs.

One day, near his death, I heard my father say how interested he was in the island of Tristan da Cunha, and that many years before he had felt God had told him to pray for that place. Years later I mentioned this in a sermon and a lady came up to me to say that her cousin's ministry in that place had been really blessed around the time my dad would have been praying. What difference does prayer make? We may never fully know the answer but we do know that God commands it. Ask him to stretch your heart.

Having asked and listened, we must *go*. If every one of us went to a third-world country just once in our life, we would never be the same again. One student who left our group to go to South America and work amongst street children found herself working with tiny children who were raped and shot, with thirteen-year-olds holding glue (to sniff) in one hand, and their baby in the other; young girls colouring in pictures on their cardboard box to make it more like home. I asked her one day, 'How do you know who to go to? There is so much need.' She replied, 'I have to ask God who it is that he has for me today'. That is all any of us have to ask.

God may not want you to be an overseas missionary but have you ever asked? Could you ask or is there just too much to lose? It is only when everything is on the altar that we can ask for God's heart for the world, because unless we are prepared to be part of the answer to our prayer there is no point in praying it! The first student I met from mainland China, many years ago, came to a meal in our house. We explained that we prayed before our meal. He said, 'Oh yes, Jesus is very popular here, I saw a picture of him in the National Gallery on two pieces of wood. Can you explain this to me?' Another student – from Turkey – told me that she had had a dream of herself, much younger, being pushed through a crowd of people. She was going to be put to death for the things she had done wrong in her life. Suddenly a man stepped out of the crowd and took her place, being put to death for her... She asked, 'Can you tell me what this means?'

My husband went to a party given by a friend from Afghanistan. When he arrived our friend announced him: 'This is my friend Nick. He's a Christian and I go to his house with international students every week.' Immediately a young Iranian man came up to him. 'Nick, are you a Christian?' As my husband nodded, he said, 'Could you explain this dream to me? I saw Jesus! I don't know how I knew it was him, but I did, and he was beautiful, I loved this man! He told me that one day I would come to him.' God does bring a witness to those he died to save, but, it says in Romans 10:14, 'How ... will they call on Him in whom they have not believed? How will they believe in Him whom they have not heard? And how will they hear without a preacher?'

Finally we must *give*. I have put giving last because it is so easy to buy ourselves out of commitment with a dollop of cash. If we inform ourselves, if we pray, go and see for ourselves, then our giving will be totally different. Le'ts ask God to stretch our hearts so we can stand in the gap for some of these places where people are dying to know that they are loved. Recently someone said to me, 'It almost seems too good to be true that someone out there loves me'. The Father's heartbroken words, passed on through Ezekiel, cry out to us across the centuries: 'I searched for a man among them who would build up the wall and stand in the gap before Me for the land, so that I would not destroy it; but I found no one'.[138]

Some years ago I visited another country and spoke about the bruise that was on God's heart as he saw the pain and weeping of our planet, and the millions going into lost eternity every minute. The group I spoke to was heartbroken. There was silence in that room for many long minutes, after I finished speaking, and all you could hear was soft weeping. Then one after another, people began to cry out to God for the area of society or the world that God had laid on their heart.

One young woman began to cry for the unborn children of that country which used abortion as a contraception. She said, 'Lord, you determined the colour of these children's hair, the colour of their eyes, their fingerprints! God have mercy on us that we treat them like garbage to be thrown away'. For many years since, this girl has been running a mother and baby home rescuing the unwanted of that society. One person prayed about the poor who were living on the rubbish dump outside the town, another for the prostitutes, another for family disintegration, another for street children, some prayed for parts of the world which were not yet reached with the gospel. The leader of the base wept as he said, 'Lord, I am so sorry that we leave compassion issues to women and children, and we men don't weep before you'. All around the room we heard the heart of God beating for his world. Will you stand in the gap?

When I was in Russia one of the girls responded to God's heart for his world by going home and kneeling by her bed, asking the Lord to speak to her. Immediately into her head came a picture of one of the little 'Babushkas', the elderly ladies who stand on every street corner, dressed in black, eyes downcast and hopeless, wordlessly holding out their hands in begging gesture. She said that as she looked at the lady in the picture, she saw Jesus standing before her with his hands stretched out, but the Babushka never lifted her eyes and would not look or listen to his pleading. Then as the girl watched, she heard cruel laughter and the enemy entered, and while the girl wept and cried out, the little lady was engulfed in flames. The next day that girl spent her day walking around the streets and the underground stations of Moscow, sitting with the old ladies, giving them food, speaking to them about the Jesus who loved them and was calling to them.

In Matthew 6, Jesus talks a lot about fool's gold! He talks about our anxieties for food and clothing (to say nothing of iPods, designer clothing and a host of other things we spend our money and time to buy). Jesus cries out to us and says this: 'Seek first [God's] kingdom and his righteousness, and all these things will be added to you'. (Well, maybe not the iPod!) Will you divide your bread with the hungry? Will you be a world-changer? If you do so, you will be given perhaps one of the most wonderful titles ever conferred by God on his people: 'The repairer of the breach, the restorer of the streets in which to dwell'.[139]

8

The Secret Wealth of Hidden Places

Mining the Seam of Suffering

I was asked to speak at an unusual evangelistic meeting recently. People had been invited by their church friends to a café to think about the subject of suffering. The invitations were covered with one-liners: 'My business collapsed and I was made bankrupt.' 'I have just learned I cannot have children.' 'My teenage son recently died tragically and suddenly.' 'I have recently been through a messy divorce.' There were a number of other lines which spoke of suffering, and of the hope that God had brought to each person in the midst of despair.

At that meeting one lady spoke briefly of her pain and what it meant to look beyond the 'why' to what she knew of God's love, and in particular of his participating in our pain by sending his own son to die. As she spoke I remembered a day when my daughter was two years old. It seemed to me that all my friends had well-behaved toddlers who walked beside them down the road. My daughter, however, was obsessed with cars. She wanted to touch them, and the moment my hand let go of hers she shot towards the road at alarming speed! One day I had to pay a bill in a tyre workshop which was on the edge of London's south circular road. I barricaded myself into the shop explaining that my daughter liked escaping, and I was in the middle of writing the cheque when suddenly everything seemed to go very quiet. She was nowhere to be seen. The man behind the counter helpfully offered that there was another door which led out into the workshop!

As I sprinted through the door I saw sparks flying everywhere but no toddler. I glanced left and saw my two-year-old racing for that incredibly busy road, the London south circular, with her arms spread wide, laughing as she raced towards certain death. I screamed (she could not hear) and covered the ground between myself and her at record speed, snatching her up as she was about to run into the busy road, my heart banging uncomfortably for what seemed like hours afterwards. If she had entered the traffic I would, without thinking, have run out after her trying to get between her and coming disaster. As I thought about that incident later I realized that the cross was like God's scream to his people. 'Stop! You will get killed if you go that way!' It was his interposing the body of his precious son between us and certain death. A Christian is not an escapist during desperate times, hiding from the pain of reality in a comfort blanket. Instead, the love and pain of the cross give a whole new dimension to our response to suffering, despite the agony we are often experiencing.

Suffering is common to humanity, it is written into the fact that we are transient, we die. We are fragile, we get sick. We are interdependent, we hurt one another. Our responses to suffering range from despair, to anger, to questioning. We say, 'It's not fair', and in that response is the assumption that if there is a God he should at least be fair, so why has he allowed this to happen? Adrian Plass wrote of a time when in anger he had questioned God at the death of a friend's baby. In his piece of prose, 'My Baby', he wrote what he felt God's reply had been.

My Baby

I wish you knew how much I love you all. I wish you could trust me as David did. You've asked me a question about the death of a baby. Now I will ask *you* some questions, and you must decide whether I've earned the right to be trusted whatever I do. My questions are about Jesus.

When he was dragged from the Garden of Gethsemane after a night of agonised prayer and terrible, lonely fear; when he was put on trial for simply being himself, and beaten, and kicked, and jeered at; did I insist that you solve for me the problem of pain? No, I let you hurt and abuse my son – my baby.

When he hauled himself, bruised and bleeding along the road to his own death, knowing that a single word from him would be enough to make me release him from his burden, did I let you down? No, I let you crush him under the weight of your cross. My son – my baby.

And when the first nail smashed into the palm of his hand, and everything in my father's heart wanted to say to those legions of weeping angels 'Go! Fight your way through and rescue him. Bring him back where he belongs', did I abandon you to judgement? No I let you kill my son – my baby.

And when he had been up on that accursed cross for three long hours, and with every ounce of strength left in his poor suffering body he screamed at *me* 'Why have you forsaken me?' did I scream back 'I haven't! I haven't! It's all just a nightmare – come back, they aren't worth it!'

No, I loved you too much – far too much to do that. I let your sin cut me off from my son – my baby.

And that death, dismal, depressing and horribly unjust as it was – the death of my innocent son, has brought peace and life to millions who've followed that same Jesus, who came back to life, back to his friends, and back to me.

Trust me, when it comes to the death of babies – believe me – I do know what I'm doing.[140]

My favourite Old Testament character is Joseph. He starts out with social advantages, love, and prophetic promise, and one can forgive him for being just a tad cocky with it! The road to fulfilling those promises, however, is very different from the one he had anticipated. I often wonder where Joseph would have been if he had experienced as many 'words from the Lord' as we do in the course of our seeking God's validation sometimes.

The road to fulfilment of God's plan for our life is often fraught with pitfalls and pain, tears and anger, and the gnawing anxiety that we have finally blown it by our frustration with God! I remember once visiting our mentor Ray, desperately hoping he would have a wonderful prophecy of glory in the midst of the darkness and pain we were experiencing. He looked us in the eye and said quietly, 'The Lord has not revealed to me how long you will have to go through this. All I know is that you are in the hand of God'. This was not the encouragement I wanted to hear at the time, but even then I respected him for not trying to give us something hopeful which he had not received from God. This was a valley we had to go through, certain of God's hand alone.

Throughout scripture we follow the following pattern: promise – death of that promise – supernatural fulfilment of the original promise! Abraham is promised a prolific family yet Sarah is barren. Abraham proceeds to do what we so often do in this time of confusion when God's word appears to be untrue for us; he makes it happen! The Arab-Israeli struggle from that time to this has been bloody and terrible evidence of trying to fulfil God's word ourselves. I have tried to 'make God's word come true' for myself many times, and the result has been disastrous, sometimes for some time to come.

Joseph's promise dies. Today we are calling and training many young people, and we promise them much. We tell them they are anointed when sometimes we mean to say they are gifted. Encouragement is vital, but not at the cost of our personal integrity. We must only ever give people what God has given us for them, no more, no less. We offer young people 'a chance to travel, to be excited, to take Jesus to the nations, winning the world for his glory'. This is something very dear to my heart, as my husband and I have sent scores of young people into short- and long-term mission. Yet when Jesus came to found a movement that would change the world, his words were incredibly stringent: 'Whoever does not carry his own cross and come after Me cannot be My disciple'.[141] The man last seen carrying his cross in Jesus' time was never seen again. In the end, we can only remain faithful for love, because power and excitement are never lasting. Churchill famously said, 'Success is seldom final, failure is seldom fatal, courage is what counts'.

I have dedicated this book to Ray Mayhew, a pastor in Omaha, Nebraska. Nick and I first knew him when he was on the leadership team of Ichthus Christian Fellowship in South London, and for some years was our mentor. Ray is an unassuming man with a pastoral heart and an extraordinary teaching ministry. Since youth he has suffered with pain in his back resulting from a lifting injury at 19. Severe scar tissue and adhesions resulted which caused the spinal nerves to 'stick' together (technically called arachnoiditis). The result is that when he moves, the nerves don't slide in their sheaths but instead cause pain and further inflammation. No event of his adult life, including his wedding, has been free from pain, and he has missed out on times playing with his children and later attending graduations. The severity of his condition increased to a place where it became incapacitating and for many years he has been unable to travel or vacation with his family away from home. Nevertheless, Ray would say that pain has not become his identity and his life is far more about joy than grief over loss. Far from dropping quietly out of service, in addition to pastoral leadership in a church in Omaha, Ray has worked on producing an exceptionally rich online resource for pastors and Christian workers including those who cannot afford training and books.[142] His insights come from a lifetime spent concentrating on Jesus. This man is fruitful and faithful in pain, disappointment (he has been prayed for many times, for healing), and in the teeth of the enemy's whispers, no doubt, that he should give up. For me, this is the kind of life that inspires me to keep on, far more than the recounting of endless 'victories', encouraging though these may be.

Joseph experienced many years between promise and fulfilment. The important thing to glean from his story is not that he stuck to his vision through thick and thin and it finally got fulfilled…we don't know if he did! He probably had many times of despair, and he certainly had no part in fulfilling the vision. The important thing for us to see is that in order for that vision to be fulfilled, Joseph had to suffer.

If we want to be conformed to Jesus' likeness (and that surely is the greatest treasure we could receive) we will have to go through pain. As we see when we are going through deserts, fool's gold glistens most at times like this. Any way out looks better than standing firm where we are. Leaving the church, leaving the family or the problem, walking away from the hurt, immersing ourselves in materialism. When asked why men become beasts when drunk, Samuel Johnson replied, 'A man makes a beast of himself to get rid of the pain of being a man'.[143] Fool's gold is found in anything that alleviates the pain of being human, rather than hiding in the arms of the creator himself.

Some years ago when we were serving God as faithfully as we knew how to, everything in our lives seemed to go wrong! It seemed that I only had to pray for something for the opposite to happen. In addition to this I felt punished. I knew that I had not been very obedient to the Lord and although I had asked his and others' forgiveness, the Accuser[144] was still giving me a hard time. I saw everything as punitive. After a long time of difficulty and sometimes of despair, someone sent me a book on not wasting times of pain, and as I read it, God spoke clearly to me. My mind was cast back to a moment some years before, when my husband and I sat down together and talked about our lack of spiritual power. Together we cried out to God for more, and through tears we said, 'No matter what it costs, and we realise it may cost everything, we want you to fill us to a far greater extent, so that your power can be seen through our lives.' The Lord spoke quietly to me as I read that morning, saying: 'You asked to be more like my son, and my son went through crucifixion'. Suddenly it was as though a light switched on! I no longer felt punished, I felt that God in his grace was answering that earlier prayer, and in so doing he was 'scooping me out' to make more room for himself.

Things did not get better! We moved three weeks later and I had the first of three miscarriages. The second miscarriage was the most difficult in some ways because it was late in the pregnancy and a baby girl was born to us, fragile as a tiny bird, only living a few minutes. I was left alone in a side ward that night, weeping. I remembered how in the past I figuratively shook my fist at God when things went wrong, and felt punished. I said, 'This time it's going to be different. I cannot look at your cross, Lord Jesus, and not know that you are love or that the Father cares'. I pulled the covers over my head and with the tears still flowing I sang a current chorus: 'Worthy, O worthy are you Lord'. The situation didn't change, but I did. Something of the King's purse dropped into my spirit that night and I have not felt impoverished or punished ever again, nor have I doubted that he is good, whatever of good or ill should come our way.

Jesus did not simply reveal the truth about God, he revealed the truth about man as he was made to be – and he suffered. In fact, 'He learned obedience from the things which He suffered'.[145] The time comes to all of us when we doubt that God is faithful because our heart is breaking, and the enemy is quick to capitalize on the situation. I have not always dealt well with these times and have watched my friends also do one of four things with suffering.

The first natural reaction is to become bitter and disillusioned. Some give up very quickly on God when things are not fixed by a simple prayer. It is worse, in a way, when we simply step back off the front line and settle for second best – it has been well said that it is easier to cool down a fanatic than to warm up a corpse! A third and really sad reaction to suffering is for the Christian to suppress their feelings, mistakenly thinking we need to be 'triumphant' at such times, and say, 'God is good, I'm fine'. This leads to gross unreality which in turn can produce depression and disillusionment. The best reaction of all is, of course, reality. When we acknowledge our pain but turn to God for his comfort, we begin to start on the road to health. There is no shame in questions and tears and even anger: he is our loving Father, and we need to go on speaking to him. Silence brings a loneliness that increases our pain fourfold.

Sometimes people have said to me that they are rather worried that they have never suffered, and expect a deluge at any point! We are not to live our lives expecting calamity; the grace is simply there for us when we need it. God's plan is not to find some special way to put us through the most pain possible. Because we live in a fallen world, and especially if we follow him, we will get hurt, but when we are in him, he works in these things to produce his likeness.

I remember praying with a young woman who had a fear of confrontation. She had known a lot of violent confrontation in her life and was reduced to a quivering jelly whenever she needed to confront or sort out anything relationally. God began to restore this woman's dignity and poise as she looked to him and made him the only one she obeyed implicitly. Isaiah 8:12–14 says '…you are not to fear what they fear or be in dread of it. It is the Lord of hosts whom you should regard as holy. And He shall be your fear, and He shall be your dread. *Then* he shall become a sanctuary'. (Italics mine.) One day this young lady, who was a teacher, told me she had been made head of discipline in her school, 'Because,' they had said to her, 'You are so good at handling confrontation'! It was never God's intention that she should have suffered as a child in that way, but God was able to redeem that situation and produce his likeness in her as she submitted her pain to him.

Sin is often the first cause of suffering to enter our heads, and some of us put everything down to our own wrongdoing. Biblically this is clearly untrue, but where sin is the cause of our pain, the cure is equally clear. In giving us free will to choose obedience to him, the Father took the biggest risk of all, the risk that we would use our freedom badly. With the entry of sin, barriers of every sort go up – between man and God, between man and man, between the sexes, and between the generations. Not that all suffering is caused by our personal sin: all over the world there are innocent victims of atrocity. I have talked to many victims of cruelty from many countries. I have talked to a young man who undoubtedly murdered many people in his warring country, after his own relatives had been murdered. We say, 'It is not fair, he was a victim of cruelty, why should he have to pay for his reactions?' We see God as punitive, whereas suffering is sometimes produced by cause and effect. Just as the natural laws take disastrous effect if we flout them (the law of gravity being a good example) so there are moral laws written into our universe, and if we flout them down we go, often with innocent people tied to us.

The first thing to harm Joseph was his family. Both our nuclear family and our spiritual family can hurt us in ways that no one else can. Joseph's nuclear family had a violent reaction to him! Part of this was the fact that he had been preferred by his father – injustice brings about estrangement, bitterness and pain in many nuclear families. Have you ever noticed that in Deuteronomy 27:12–13, the tribes of Israel are divided into two groups? One half of the tribes declare God's blessings and the other half declare his curse. The thing is, apart from Reuben who forfeited his birthright by immorality, the tribes who have to declare the curse are all the sons of concubines, while those declaring blessing are the legitimate sons. The 'illegitimate tribes' may well have seen their position as unfair, or that God considered them of lesser status.

In the New Testament, however, we see the Son of God deliberately seek out the victims of unfair situations. Have you noticed how Jesus deliberately approached the people who would naturally be excluded by Old Testament law from parts of the Temple? In Matthew's Gospel the first person Jesus is reported as healing was a leper, completely excluded from worshipping among the people of God. Next he is recorded as healing a Gentile, who could only come into the very outermost court of the house of God. The third person Matthew describes as being healed by Jesus was a woman – she would have been confined to the women's court and unable to receive teaching in his day. Jesus deliberately broke down every 'dividing wall'[146] and made a way for those from an unfair position to come into a place of equality and grace.

Joseph's family did not just snub or laugh at him. They hated him violently enough to sell him into slavery! I constantly speak to people whose family have abused or harmed them in such a way that they are enslaved. One young girl I met continually sought to gain the attention of men by sexual advances. I asked her one day why she behaved the way she did around the opposite sex and she told me a tale repeated by many others. Her father had preferred her brothers, had set high standards for her to achieve, and even when she got A grades, would ask about the things she could have improved in. She tried to excel at sport, so that she could be like her brothers, but her father never noticed. 'I have to do something to get men's attention,' she said sadly. This story, of course, is mild compared with the tales of pain and abuse we hear all around us. How can God turn slavery to freedom for us? How can we reject the fool's gold of bitterness and vindictiveness that rises in our hearts?

Contrary to popular opinion I doubt very much that Joseph was totally saintly for those years of slavery! I am sure that self-pity would have reared its head. How often he must have cried out, 'It's not fair! Surely I did not deserve this situation'. Revenge would have followed: 'If ever I get out of this hole I'll make them pay'. What happened in those years of pain, rejection, injustice, loneliness and despair to turn Joseph to forgiveness and a righteous perspective that led him to say: 'God meant it for good'?[147]

First of all Joseph got to a place where he knew himself. Suffering and pressure show us who we really are. I was speaking to a friend about the fact that suffering 'scoops you out' ready for more of God to fill you, and he replied, 'How is that possible? When I'm suffering I become the most unpleasant person alive! Despair, self-pity, and anger bust out of me, and in fact I am far more self-centred at such a time, not less'. I agreed that this was my experience too, but at the end of it I knew myself better than ever before.

With the apostle Paul I have to say 'nothing good dwells in me',[148] and at that point I am ready to ask God to fill and change me again. Once I have learned to face myself, I am less likely to blame others. Some people never do face themselves. For them, everything is always someone else's fault, and maturing and changing into Christ's likeness is always difficult. But God's refining does not leave us guilty and condemned. Instead it frees us to be able to forgive another for being flawed, and as time goes by, his faithfulness helps us to gain perspective.

Gavin Reid, then the Bishop of Maidstone, interviewed a seventeen-year-old who was being confirmed. He said to the lad, 'How is it that you believe that God is good? I happen to know that out of your seventeen years, you have spent thirteen of them in hospital. Surely that isn't fair, is it?' The young man did not know the question was coming, but without blinking he replied, 'No, sir, it isn't fair, but he has all eternity to put it right!'

Our family (regardless of their faith or lack of it) can hurt and reject us. We may respond with 'martyrdom', feeling that we are always the victim, or we may react in anger and aggression. Joseph's life encourages us to look at the very hurt we have gone through, to accept it from God, acknowledging that the pain grieves him but that he can bring good from it. God speaks through the prophet Joel: 'Then I will make up to you for the years that the swarming locust has eaten, the creeping locust, the stripping locust and the gnawing locust, My great army which I sent among you'.[149] It is only when we get to the point of acknowledging that our life is in his hands no matter what we have to face, that we can hear from him how to respond lovingly to those who have hurt us.

Then again, it is possible that it is our church family that has hurt us. Jesus is clearly hurt when he heals ten lepers and only one of them returns to give glory to God. After a talk on suffering, the crowd melts quietly away, unable to take the reality of discipleship, and Jesus says wistfully to the disciples, 'Will you also go away?' Because we are flawed and human, we, the family of God, will criticize or use people, we will let them down. How are we going to respond like Joseph if we are on the other end of these injustices? After all those years to feed on his grievances, he meets his brothers with a feast!

In addition to knowing ourselves, and forgiving others

for as long as it takes, there is another thing we must do: we need to learn to build altars. In the Old Testament, every time the Lord comes and meets his people, altars are built. Following Jesus means building a table of sacrifice (many times!) – laying down our rights to our time, to our being loved, our being respected, to every part of our life, over and over again. Only then are we able to feast with others at that table.

His family were not the only ones to harm Joseph. Some of his hardship was the result of his own weakness. At seventeen Joseph was big-headed, immature, disrespectful and a tell-tale. Not major flaws, perhaps, but they led to major problems! I often go to extraordinary lengths to prove (at least to myself) that things are not my fault. Of course when that is right, the accuser, Satan, still tries to make us uncomfortable and we need to speak out God's grace at such times, but there are many times when we are simply hiding from the truth and the Lord cannot bring us into hope while we are in denial. I may tell you that I am just an insignificant servant of Jesus, but woe betide you if you tell *me* that! Sometimes we are falsely accused – a criticism may not be accurate, but what rises in my heart when someone criticizes me is often the attitude that God wants to deal with.

Often it is our own sins or weaknesses that lead to situations of pain and until we acknowledge that, we cannot be helped or healed. Dom Helda Camara, the Archbishop of Recife and Olinda in Brazil, said, 'Being holy means getting up immediately every time you fall, with humility and joy. It doesn't mean never falling into sin. It means being able to say, "Yes Lord I have fallen a thousand times. But thanks to you I have got up again a thousand and one times"'.[150] If we do not admit our own sins or mistakes, the promises God made over our lives may never be fulfilled – every promise has a condition in scripture. Similarly if we admit our weaknesses too easily we cannot avail ourselves of the wonder of the cross. I am a hopelessly flawed human being and without Jesus I would never make it. However, I am not content with that, I am, like the apostle Paul, 'determined to know nothing among you except Jesus Christ, and Him crucified'.[151] I want to know the cross in my life, putting self to death so that even in weakness his will is done in my life. The gospel proclaims reality! It acknowledges that we are flawed and that our life will not be victory all the way. We will fall, we will let each other and God down. But the great news is that in repentance, in confession, in facing the truth for as long as it takes, we are transformed into his likeness!

Circumstances were unfair for Joseph. His brothers' reaction to him was more violent than he could have expected, and the situation with Potiphar's wife was terribly unjust. He had been trying to honour his master and to remain godly and he was plunged into injustice and cruelty. Many circumstances can plunge us into despair – losing a secure employment, unexpected cruelty, sickness, depression and bereavement. We stake our lives on God being fair; what do we do when things are simply inexplicable?

We know that because of sin, because of Satan, because of a flawed world, unfair things do happen to good people. If you have been taught that followers of God will be healthy and wealthy you just need to read the book of Job. To say 'Why me?' or 'Why them?' when tragedy strikes means we think that good things are a reward from God, yet 'He ... sends rain on the righteous and the unrighteous'.[152] By being born into a fallen world we are subject to the injustices of its ruler,[153] yet by being reborn into the kingdom of light, we can expect redemption of the very worst that can happen to us!

Neglect causes suffering. Our poor stewardship of the earth can cause natural and physical disasters. In the tsunami of 2004, there was an interesting debate in one of the UK newspapers. Some religious leaders had said that people would find it hard to believe in God during this time. 'Nonsense', said the secular journalists! In their experience, they wrote, suffering causes people to examine the bigger questions of life, and gave far more impetus to a search for God. 'Only a very fragile and dimwitted faith would be shaken by an event that was just the latest in a series of natural disasters – earthquakes, volcanic eruptions, hurricanes and tsunamis – stretching back to the dawn of time', wrote Tom Utley in the *Daily Telegraph*. 'An event such as the tsunami is a heaven-sent – or perhaps hell-sent – opportunity for church leaders... to grab our attention and to tell us what it all means'![154] We are sometimes too quick to try to find a soft answer to major questions but these very questions can lead to a sense of living in a moral universe created by a God who exists and cares.

Joseph's circumstances were unexplained. We know now that God used Joseph's training in administration of Potiphar's household, and then in administration of the jail, to prepare him to administer a nation; that he used his pain to bring blessing, forgiveness and redemption to God's people. Yet at the time Joseph had no possible clue as to why he was going through the pain. What answer would help the mother whose little girl was raped, what hope do we give the relatives of a murder victim? Trite answers will not help us here. You can bet Joseph asked 'Why?'. I have often been so comforted that Jesus on the cross asked, 'Why have you forsaken me?'. 'Why?' is not the end of faith but a natural response to suffering.

Many years ago a student came to see me. She told me something she had told no one else at the university, and it cost her a lot to say it. Her mother had suffered with depression for many years and even when she was a tiny girl first at school the girl remembered worrying about leaving her mother at home. Just as she was preparing to take her GCSEs, her mother committed suicide in a particularly gruesome way. She said to me, 'If only I knew why this had happened I could maybe move on. Because I don't know the answer, I am afraid I will do the same one day and it haunts me.' My only excuse for what happened next is that I was a lot younger and very inexperienced in these matters. My husband had just returned home and I briefly told him what had happened, and we sat her down, prayed with her and let her go, with very little understanding that she had just opened a can of worms which could overwhelm her.

Fortunately the Lord was gracious to her, despite our inexperience. She went back to her college bedroom and cried until she fell into an exhausted sleep. That night she had a dream in which she said everything sad that had ever happened to her (going back to when she was very small) played out in front of her eyes like a film. She said there were events that she had forgotten, and the large traumas including her mother's death. However, she said, as she was watching these events she felt safe, surrounded by light and warmth which she somehow knew was the presence of God. Suddenly the 'film' replayed again, but this time it showed all the happy events of her life, again including things she had forgotten long ago. At the end, the Lord spoke to her and he said very simply, 'I was with you during all the pain you encountered during your life. Now these are the memories that are to fill your mind from now on.' I almost did not recognize the girl who hurtled down the road on her bicycle the next day and practically fell off at my feet, so great was her haste to tell me what had happened! Her face was shining with joy, and a peace that she had never shown previously. The answer as to why these things had happened never fully came, but the presence and love of God and the fact that he was there brought her the strength and hope to move forward.

When Jacob thought he had lost his son, he appears to have given up hope, living as a broken old man from whom we hear no faith or hope. Joseph, on the other hand, seems to have a buoyancy that reached beyond the circumstances to what he knew of God in spite of the pain.

In addition to family difficulties, our own weakness, and harmful personal circumstances, direct evil is a very real cause of suffering, as we see in the book of Job. Job is not told why misfortune and bereavement came to him. We know that there was war in heaven and the enemy had taunted God with Job's faithfulness, attributing this to the fact that Job had known God's smile and blessing. God's vote of confidence in Job meant his allowing the enemy to test him, but Job had no means of knowing that this was the case. Unlike us so often, Job chose to keep speaking to God. Certainly he shook his fist in despair and wished he had never been born, but he never took the option of turning his back on God, retreating into silence, or doubting his existence. His choice to risk love and life once more came when God spoke to him after seeming endless silence. The loudness of our grief drowns out the voice of God sometimes, but the day will dawn when we hear his whisper again, and hope returns.

God's silence is perhaps one of the most testing things of all in our suffering. The Bible says of his dealings with Hezekiah, 'God left him alone only to test him, that He might know all that was in his heart.' [155]

After Joseph utters that wonderful faith-filled statement, 'Do not dreams belong to God?' he remains two more years in prison! One day I read Satan's taunting words to God in Job 1:9: 'Does Job fear you for nothing?' The words challenged me at a time when I felt unwell and without a lot of hope for the future. I realized I served God *for* things: to be loved, to be in his presence, and for a whole host of less worthy things too. I cried out to God that day and said, 'Lord I want to serve you for nothing! Whatever happens to me for good or ill, I want to serve you because you are worthy of the best I have, even if I never hear from you again in this lifetime'. Immediately I had release from that nagging question 'Why?'.

In his brilliant book *When Heaven Is Silent*, Ronald Dunn speaks about living in the light of Romans 8:28, that all things really do 'work together for good for those who love God and are called according to his purpose'.[156] He says that after a time of anger, silence, questions and all the attendant emotions produced by pain and loss, the Christian moves from 'Why?' to 'What next?' The dawn may take a long while to come, but its golden promise will rise once more. My mother lived her life faithfully towards

God, but in old age she suffered from dementia and a day came when she was mistakenly given too high a dosage of medication. As a result she was sectioned and sent to a psychiatric hospital. I was devastated for her and rang her that evening, worrying about her confusion and pain. She was indeed outraged and upset at being somewhere unfamiliar where she did not feel safe. 'But,' she said to me, 'It says in the Word that "all things work together for good, to those who love him" and I am looking for the jewel, the person I can lead to him in this place.' This woman of God was having problems with her mind, she had been through unexpected trauma and fear, but she had treasure stored up against a day of disaster!

The outcome for Joseph is the same as the outcome for us – true provision from the King's purse. Joseph tells his brothers, 'You meant evil against me, but God meant it for good'.[157] The story of Peter's challenge and reinstatement by Jesus on the beach in John 21 comes directly in the middle of two life-changing events for the apostle. Two pages before John 21, in my Bible, we find the story of Peter's denial, the darkest time in his life. Two pages later comes Acts 2 and Pentecost! A man who loved his Lord but constantly failed was moved into his destiny by coming to know himself so well that he relied only upon Jesus from that time onwards. After Calvary comes resurrection. Psalm 30:5 says, 'Weeping may last for the night, But a shout of joy comes in the morning.' Genesis 1:5 says, 'There was evening and there was morning'. God always ends in morning! Our life's work may seem to have crashed into dust, our dearest hope may lie in the grave, weeping and pain may consume us for a time, but deep inside the Christian sounds, like a clarion, the resurrection promise: the best is yet to come.

To deny pain is not faith, and it never brings true wealth. As we express anguish to God and, where possible, to the right people, we are free to choose to worship not in unreality but in deepening faith. At this point, while a time of worship may not yet touch our heart, our worship touches heaven.

You may wish to come right now to the King whose treasure is so painfully gained, and commit afresh to seeking hidden wealth in secret places.

'Lord Jesus, I want to commit afresh to you. In the light of your cross and all that it meant for you, but also all that it means for me, I choose to take it up and follow you.

I acknowledge my frailty to you, Lord. I know that anything I say to you now, I may take back in a moment of pain. But I purpose to serve you, Lord Jesus, through all the changes that life may bring me. I choose to serve you when things are going well, and I have advancement and joy, and I choose to serve you when the storm breaks or I cannot see my way. When life seems unfair, and you seem far away, I ask you to remind me of this moment and my choice to follow.

I commit to you in the sure and certain faith that you are good and that you love me and those whom I love, and that all things will work together for good to those who love you. If, in order to fulfil your promise to me, you need to mould and melt me, I accept the cross in faith that you will make me like Joseph's second son

Ephraim, fruitful, not because of my affliction but right there in it.

Thank you that you were a 'man of sorrows and acquainted with grief'[158] and yet you were also 'anointed … with … joy'.[159] I trust my life into your hands and ask that I will not seek fool's gold and easy satisfaction, but the lasting treasure of your face, mirrored in my own.

Amen.

9

What is Real?

Holy Club or Loving Community

"'What is REAL?" asked the Rabbit one day...
"Does it mean having things that buzz inside
you and a stick-out handle?"

"Real isn't how you are made," said the Skin
Horse. "It's a thing that happens to you. When
a child loves you for a long, long time, not just
to play with but REALLY loves you, then you
become Real."

"Does it hurt?" asked the Rabbit.

"Sometimes," said the Skin Horse, for he
was always truthful. "When you are Real you
don't mind being hurt."

"Does it happen all at once, like being wound
up," he asked, "or bit by bit?"

"It doesn't happen all at once," said the Skin
Horse. "You become. It takes a long time. That's
why it doesn't happen often to people who break
easily, or have sharp edges, or who have to be
carefully kept. Generally, by the time you are

Real, most of your hair has been loved off, your eyes drop out and you get loose in the joints and very shabby. But these things don't matter at all, because once you are Real you can't be ugly, except to people who don't understand."[160]

Do you wish there were more people with whom you could be real? The whole unvarnished edition of who you are, with no cover-ups or attempts at fitting in; with no fear of judgment?

Gerald Coates speaks about three stages to be found in true relationship, at least in Western society.[161] The first stage is veneer, where we do our best to engage the other person's interest and respect. We take them at face value and often think they are perfect, despite knowing ourselves and the fact that we are all heir to human weakness. Then, needless to say, we move swiftly into stage two of a relationship – disillusionment! We begin to see flaws in the other person and, forgetting our own, we become disillusioned with them. This is often compounded by the number of relationships we have had where we have been disappointed. If we last long enough in relationship with that person there is a chance for stage three to set in – reality. This involves a choice to commit to one another, aware that we are all flawed and failing human beings, but with the help of God and of each other, we may improve!

I find the concept of these three stages so helpful. We who are part of the body of Christ ought to be the most 'real', the most transparent of all people, yet the cost is great, and most of us settle back into a form of relationship that keeps reality at bay. The problem with this life choice, of course, is twofold. First, we will fall out with one another far more frequently because we have never embraced the reality of who we are.

Secondly, if we are not real we will never be free to move on, or to change into the likeness of Jesus. The story is told that when Michelangelo was still an impoverished sculptor, rumour had it that a large piece of marble lay discarded on the hillside because a flaw had been discovered running right through the centre of it. Michelangelo spent the night on the hillside, so that when the sun rose he could see the flaw as the rays struck the marble. As he looked at the flaw, the storyteller goes on to say (probably with some poetic licence!) that he saw in his mind's eye the great curved back of the David, his most famous statue.

When we have acknowledged that we are flawed, then we can see beyond the cracks to what we may become. Similarly, when we meet flaws in others, like Michelangelo with his piece of flawed marble, and like God with his flawed children, we can see what they may become. Only a realistic view can free us to do this. Anything else is wishful thinking and fool's gold.

Once when I was visiting Romania I met a remarkable young woman. She was in her early twenties and had three young children. On my last day there, I said I was catching the plane that afternoon and she came to me begging me not to go. I explained that I had to, and that I needed to join my family. She replied, 'It's just that no one has ever loved me like you have'. Now this might sound plausible if you did not know the whole story. I had been there precisely a week, I had met and prayed with each person on the discipleship school, and had spent precisely half an hour with this girl, listening to her and praying with her! The thing was, no one had ever focused on her and loved her long enough to free her to be real before. I had been with her half an hour!

She then said something that has stayed with me over the years. 'Can I ask you one thing? Why have you taken so long to come to us?'

Her farewell gift to me was a stick of wood with a blackened hole in its side that she had nailed upright so that the point reached heavenwards. 'This represents my life,' she told me. 'I have flaws in me, but I am still stretching up to reach out towards God.'

The Lord spoke to me that day through that young woman. What is it that takes us so long to go to those who need love and freedom and reality? There are many answers. We are often already too busy with the things that crowd our life. We are afraid that we will be drowned by the need. We are afraid that our flaws will show. Yet the King's purse-strings are immediately untied when people begin to form a community, based in reality, that reaches outwards. Anyone joining them breathes more freely, and realizes very quickly that this is a place where they can grow and expand because there is no value judgment going on, simply acceptance. That is not to say challenges will not be made or faced, but they are made without criticism.

I find reality perhaps the most difficult of all the treasures that God is holding out to me. It is so much easier to hide behind veneer, or – once that has been pierced – simply to walk away. It is difficult to let others see that I have pettinesses and weaknesses that I am struggling with the help of God to overcome. Surely I can do a lot of good to people without letting them too close? Well yes, that may be possible, but the strain begins to tell!

Over the years that I have sought to serve God, and have prayed with others who equally passionately desire to serve him, I have seen many people struggle for reality, and others (including myself at times) who have succumbed to the terrible strain of keeping up appearances. It is so difficult to get the balance, isn't it, between looking upwards, looking outwards and looking inwards? In a postmodern society the latter is certainly easiest! Most of us are no strangers to looking inwards, but it is when we look up into the accepting, loving eyes of our Father that we can accept the challenge to form real relationships, and to respond to the occasional whisper that our behaviour has been ungodly or immature. At that point we become free to look outwards to those who need inclusive love and acceptance.

If leaders find it hard to be real, how will those following them fare? There are many models of leadership to be seen in the Old Testament: prophet, priest, judge, soldier, and king, to name but a few. However, in the New Testament the models change dramatically to shepherd, father, brother, friend, and servant. These are far more relational images, and therefore far more difficult to follow. If I were Jesus I might have left out the line 'No longer do I call you servants ... but ... friends'![162] Servants do what you tell them, friends ask why! A friend comes close enough to challenge us.

Sometimes the people we serve do not want their leaders to have flaws either, because they want someone on a pedestal, usefully remote; someone they can aspire to but who is so far above them that their holiness is unattainable! This attitude is dangerous for anyone in leadership – people like a hero and we like to be one!

This puts inevitable strain on us to keep up appearances, because without Jesus we can never be the person everyone seems to want us to be. People loved Jesus' miracles, but when he went to Nazareth, where he was known as 'just the carpenter's son from down the road', people got angry. Why? Because the nearer we come to someone, the more real they are, the greater the challenge of their life!

When I was a little girl, my parents took Sabbath observance very seriously, and one of the few forms of acceptable recreation was to read improving Christian books! The books, on the whole, were written in the heroic style adopted by believers in bygone eras, and the heroes and heroines of faith were depicted as uniformly saintly from their earliest years upwards... I hated them! It came as a great relief later on to read the Bible and discover real people who toiled and doubted and fell but who, in restoration, were used to change the world.

We *need* to see one another close up, under pressure, in difficulties or bereavement or pain, because when we fall and rise again and keep going, when we chase after God no matter how many times we fall, that is a far greater challenge than the wonderful, remote 'saint' who never falters. That image of the saint may keep the hero alive but not the reality, because brokenness is God's way! Hiding from it simply is fool's gold. The 'foolishness' of the cross[163] and the stigma attached to Pentecost[164] both show that God's ways are not our ways. Paul positively delights in weakness,[165] that Christ's power may be seen more radiantly in his creatures.

Reality is not best served by our getting up before a large body of people and telling them in detail what unpleasant people we are. It is seen in first being real with a few, maybe only one to start with. Perhaps one of the most potent weapons against the evil one is a small group of people, a house group or cell group that has learned to be real, to accept one another for who we are. 'Ar', one of the Hebrew words in the Old Testament for 'enemy', can be translated 'one who watches'. We feel uncomfortable around some people because we feel they are always watching us to catch us out. When we are a community who accept one another we are then free to invite others to join us. This kind of 'blurred edge' group can be somewhere that is comfortable not just for Christians, but a place where people who do not yet have a faith can feel accepted and relaxed. In several churches I know, groups of like-minded people meet together, whether they are women who work from home, people interested in political issues, or other interests. The groups are a healthy mixture of those who have a living and vibrant faith, and those who, as yet, would not say they have faith in Jesus Christ at all. Reality and community is what binds the group together and makes it much easier to then share faith.

If we set out to reach people by this means without having learned a degree of reality in our home relationships or our church family relationships, the cracks will inevitably show, so we need God's help if we are to work out our life together! As the Skin Horse told the Rabbit, 'It doesn't happen all at once... you become.' I have found that it is only of limited benefit for me to spend too much inward-looking time on what is unreal about me. I ask God to show me clearly anything that is unreal about my relationships or behaviour, and ask him to continue to make my conscience sharp to his whisper, when I am withdrawing from reality with others. This obedience frees me to begin to look outwards and not to stay in an introverted huddle, never noticing or caring for those who pass by.

Why was the early church so attractive? Because they 'had all things in common; and they began selling their property and possessions and were sharing them with all, as anyone might have need. Day by day continuing with one mind in the temple, and breaking bread from house to house, they were taking their meals together with gladness and sincerity of heart'.[166]

We sometimes get hung up in trying to make our modern concepts of church conform too literally to the model in the book of Acts so that we substitute form for heart-calling. These people were attractive not necessarily because they all lived in the same house but because all that they had belonged to one another! They were utterly open. We in the UK have imbibed with our mother's milk the concept that an Englishman's home is his castle and the drawbridge goes up as we enter our front door. This has both personal and social implications. Personally, we cannot get closer to home than our own heart. Just as we shut the door on our neighbours as we walk in, so we can shut out all intrusion in terms of our personal life. I am not advocating wearing our hearts on our sleeves for all to read and spurn if they wish, but for us to have an awareness of the guards which spring up over our lifetime.

One of the most heartrendingly touching things about a baby's smile is its unguarded giving. A baby has no mask or caution to hide behind; it sees a familiar face and beams! It is sad as we watch the guards go up on that open little countenance, as life goes on. When we come into the family of God, his intention is that we are restored to Adam's freedom, which was only lost when he sinned. Some of the most pain-filled words in the Bible are to be found in Genesis 3:9: 'Then the Lord God called to the man, and said to him "Where are you?"'

From being naked and unashamed,[167] Adam and Eve began covering up: hiding from God and covering themselves from the eyes of others. By the end of chapter 3 of Genesis they had invented all sorts of things to shield them from the nakedness of just being creatures created for freedom and openness. It is part of the gospel to be real! Inherent in Christ's redemption is restoration to clarity of life. I was walking up the street one day with a mature student who had recently found Christ. He said to me, 'You know what the best thing is? I am free to be myself! I can't remember a time when I wasn't trying to be someone else, and copying them. But finding someone who completely knows me and completely loves me means I can finally be myself and I love it!' How tragic when the church becomes the one place where we *cannot* be ourselves.

Because 'stuff happens', we may need prayer and healing from God in many areas before we feel we can attempt to bring down our personal drawbridge. As we have seen in the section on wounding, the whole plan of redemption is that we move forward into reality, however, and do not quickly grab our rags of self-protection back around us the moment we get hurt again. We, the people of God, must claim our inheritance from the King's purse, and begin to reclaim our inheritance of being open and unashamed. It is terribly costly at times, but it is our only hope.

I received a letter from a young girl who had just started her first job. She wrote:

'I think the first thing I noticed when I started work was how different I felt to everyone else. I leaned totally on my Christian life and friends which was a good thing but it made me aware how different the attitudes were of my new colleagues. After working only a couple of weeks I found it was quite a struggle not to compromise when people around me don't worry about bad language, small lies, ill-humoured jokes, gossiping – things that seem very small. It was so hard not to let these attitudes slip into my own life. After a short time of working there I didn't feel different any more, which is when it dawned on me that although I should be able to relate to people my heart's attitudes should always be different.

'I realized that people won't see that I'm a Christian by me frantically trying to mention Jesus in conversations, but instead by living such a radical Christian lifestyle that people can visibly see the life of Jesus in me. In my life this means I need to avoid all gossip... I am determined to remain in God's peace when I am surrounded by chaos, and I think the most important thing for me is to be completely real; to admit I have failings and problems too, but to share how I as a Christian go about coming to a solution. I love the saying "Preach the gospel at all times; if necessary, use words".'

Our social drawbridge is certainly raised much of the time! When my husband and I first got married we lived

round the corner from a little church entirely hidden from
prying eyes by the enormous walls which encircled it. A
tiny poster exhorting us to salvation was stuck on a stick
which poked out over the top of the wall! We felt sad every
time we passed that place because it said as loudly as it
could, 'Come in here and hide from the world!'

A few years later we became involved with many
overseas students who had come to study in the UK. One
day we invited a Nigerian man home to Sunday dinner
with us. I will never forget the way he walked round and
round our tiny living room, examining everything. He
turned to us, beaming, and said, 'At last I can write home
and say I have been inside an English home! I have been
here four years, and sometimes Christians put on dinners
for us at church, but I have never been inside an English
home. In my country, you cannot say you have a friend
unless you have been into their home.' We hung our heads
in shame.

As the world gets smaller with the use of the Internet,
it also begins to stretch further away from us. Virtual
relationships are taking the place of reality. Office memos
have to be sent out exhorting people to talk to the person
at the next desk rather than sending them emails! We are
becoming like C.S. Lewis's depiction of hell in *The Great
Divorce*,[168] people so alienated from one another that if
someone moved into their street, they had to move away,
and keep moving further and further out from one another.
This is the exact opposite of God's intention in Genesis,
and it is the people of God who have to find creative ways
to rediscover community where people are free to be
themselves, yet free to change. There is no one formula
which, if we copy it, will mean we have cracked the art of

community. We simply have to start with personal reality, and then to seek God as to where to begin reaching others around us who are locked into darkness.

We know that evangelism primarily is about *being* good news, not bashing people over the head with it, yet the evangelical church has sometimes forgotten what this is all about. Being good news is about loving people. After three years spent with Jesus and nearly sixty more to think about it, the apostle John wrote the epistles of love. Of course, we can meet churches that emphasize these scriptures in order to embrace liberal theology and say that nothing matters but love – never mind the pursuit of holiness. But perhaps in the evangelical corner, while we may have our doctrines on toast, we have sometimes forgotten how to simply love people. D.L. Moody said, 'Out of a hundred people, one person may read the Bible, but ninety-nine will read Christians'. Words are important, but life is far more so. When people look at the family of God and see true, loving (albeit flawed) community, they will long for true gold.

One year when we held an outreach using a coffee shop in the evening, an off-duty policeman was passing one night, and he glanced inside. 'Christians!' he thought scornfully. He had once followed Christ but things had gone wrong in his life and he had distanced himself as far as possible from the people of faith. However, something impelled him to enter the shop. He looked at all the eager students in their yellow T-shirts, and suppressing a shudder sat down next to a safe-looking older lady. As they began to talk she told him of her life-long struggle with manic depression, how she frequently had to have periods in the psychiatric ward of the local hospital, but how God in his goodness constantly cared for her. That night the policeman went home, knelt down at his bedside, and began his journey home to the Father's arms. Reality got to him!

Another time I was telephoned by a girl whose engagement had just been broken off. Her fiancé had said that he did not think God wanted them to marry and she was saying, 'Grace, I love God so much, why doesn't he like me? What's wrong with me?' We talked about God's love in the midst of pain and after a while I said, 'You shouldn't be on your own, can you get someone to stay with you?' She replied that her housemate, who at that time had no faith, was sitting beside her as she called me. I thought afterwards that this is what being real is all about! The people of God are free to question and weep, in front of their friends, yet still show their trust in a Father who cares. I know of no better evangelism in the world!

We have looked at a journey to personal reality and also the need for corporate reality. This is something we keep having to revisit in our lives, as the trigger for our drawbridge seems very sensitive, and it snaps up very quickly again! We fail ourselves, our God and one another, and it is far easier to step back and withdraw than to pay the price of real relationships. Many of us have been failed by the 'community of saints', and decide we need a faith that is private and personal and which does not involve us in the messy business of interrelationship once more. The problem is that we were not created to be in isolation, so when we withdraw our faith will suffer rather than expand. The King's purse is found open amongst his family, and costly as recommitment may be for us, it is the only way forward in personal faith and in reaching a world in need.

Most people are very quick to smell hypocrisy. We do not need to appear perfect to those looking on, we need to be obviously real yet desperate to change into his likeness. As we are quick to apologize, tenacious in renewing broken relationships, determined to put right our wrongs, so we become a family in the best sense of the word. Ray Mayhew, in his article 'The Father's House', points out that the Hebrew word 'bayit', translated 'temple' in the Old Testament, is simply the word for house:

> 'A house, or a home, is the epicenter of family relationships, and not just religious activity. In traditional societies the home has always represented intimacy, camaraderie, hospitality, philanthropy, laughter, children, education, and even industry – the farm or workshop often being an extension of the house. 'Bayit' is … a much warmer and wider word than the English word 'temple'. It signifies that God has taken up residence in Israel and they are now learning to be at home with him.'[169]

We need to recapture this lovely sense of being the house of God. Peter tells us we are the living stones that make up this house. It is a place of warmth, fun, reality and safety, a home such as we visit in many of the warmer countries of the world whose front door is always open, and whose hospitality is unquestionable. As we do this, we will no longer be a holy club which people fear joining but an attractive living organism constantly changing and developing, free to fail and yet reflecting the glory of our Father's likeness.

10

A God-Possessed People

Uncut Stone

'And coming to Him as to a living stone which has been rejected by men, but is choice and precious in the sight of God, you also, as living stones, are being built up as a spiritual house for a holy priesthood, to offer up spiritual sacrifices acceptable to God through Jesus Christ.

For this is contained in Scripture:

"Behold, I lay in Zion a choice stone, a precious corner stone, and he who believes in Him will not be disappointed."

This precious value, then, is for you who believe; but for those who disbelieve,

"The stone which the builders rejected, this became the very corner stone,"

and,

"a stone of stumbling and a rock of offence".

They stumble because they are disobedient to the word, and to this doom they were also appointed.

But you are a chosen race, a royal priesthood, a holy nation, a people for God's own possession, so that you may proclaim the excellencies of Him who has called you out of darkness into His marvellous light; for you once were not a people, but now you are the people of God; you had not received mercy, but now you have received mercy. Beloved, I urge you as aliens and strangers to abstain from fleshly lusts which wage war against the soul. Keep your behaviour excellent among the Gentiles, so that in the thing in which they slander you as evildoers, they may because of your good deeds, as they observe them, glorify God in the day of visitation.'[170]

In *The Voyage of the Dawn Treader*, C.S. Lewis writes of a deserted island, visited by King Caspian of Narnia with Edmund, Lucy and Eustace, the three children from our world. They stumble across a stream in which lies a solid gold statue, and in trying to prod it, they discover that everything touching the water immediately turns to gold. The truth slowly dawns on them:

"'The king who owned this island," said Caspian slowly, and his face flushed as he spoke, "Would soon be the richest of all the kings of the world. I claim this land forever as a Narnian possession... It shall be called Goldwater Island." ...

"Who are you talking to?" said Edmund. "I'm no subject of yours. If anything it's the other way round. I am one of the four ancient sovereigns of Narnia and you are under allegiance to the High King, my brother."

"So it has come to that, King Edmund, has it?" said Caspian, laying his hand on his sword hilt…

Across the grey hillside above them… without noise, and without looking at them, and shining as if he were in bright sunlight though the sun had in fact gone in, passed with slow pace the hugest lion that human eyes have ever seen… They looked at one another like people waking from sleep.

"What were we talking about?" said Caspian. "Have I been making rather an ass of myself?"

"Sire," said Reepicheep, "This is a place with a curse on it. Let us go back on board at once. And if I might have the honour of naming this island, I should call it Deathwater."[171]

We have looked at a number of things which prove to be fool's gold in our lives, things that would drown us as surely as the man who swam long ago in that death-fated water and became a statue covered in gold. Every other obsession in our lives will surely drown us. It will crush the life of the Spirit out of us in the end, because we were made to run on that life of the Spirit of God. The only safe obsession, if we can put it that way, is our absorption with God himself.

The apostle Peter understandably has stones in

his mind when he writes his epistles. Simon the disciple receives a new name from Jesus, in Matthew 16, and is called Peter (Petros), the Greek word for stone. The passage quoted at the start of 1 Peter 2 is arguably one of the clearest and most beautiful descriptions of the church in the Bible, and the key phrase is in verse 9: 'You are… that you may be'. The purpose of the bride of Christ is not that she amasses beautiful buildings, gets obsessed by the length of the services or the quality of the exegesis, important as that is. The church is not, of course, an end in itself – its purpose – the entire purpose of the people of God here on earth – is to reveal Jesus. Anything that thwarts this mission is 'deathwater' to us!

Peter quotes Isaiah 28:16 (NIV): 'I lay a stone in Zion … a precious cornerstone'. A cornerstone is variously interpreted as the capstone of the building, the visible coping, or the stone at the corner of two foundation walls, which if taken out would decimate the entire building. Peter refers to Jesus as 'precious'. What makes a stone precious? Usually the rarity of a stone or metal determines its value, and Jesus the only Son of the Father is unique in his value. The extraordinary thing is that when we come to him, by divine alchemy he turns us into living stones of rare value in a world whose values are skewed and twisted by the evil one. These are the stones which build the church, the 'ekklesia', the body of believers which is to change the world and provide a living shelter to those in danger from the storms of life.

Peter should know! He was a very ordinary, fallible, flawed fisherman, whom Jesus knew, called and changed, and whose life is still impacting us thousands of years later! We waste such precious time squabbling inside the walls of our shining edifices to man's skill, but it is us, flawed and fallible as we are, who are to be evidence of true wealth and value to our society. There is absolutely nothing glamorous about being a brick in the wall, as the band Pink Floyd pointed out some years ago.

The reason we forget our position is often due to our relationship with the Lord becoming merely functional. We love him because he does things for us, or he is things to us, and we reserve the right to berate him if he does not do these things, and in so doing we miss the wonder that angels gasp at and fall before. Once we get back to loving and serving him for who he is, we begin to understand and fulfil our task here on earth, and to produce a structure that reveals his glory as the moon reflects the sun's rays. As he is faithful to us, we reflect faithfulness into our society; as he forgives, so we forgive; as he loves, so we show increased compassion, and light spreads outwards.

I have a friend who struggles with the whole concept of Jesus being a stone that people stumble over. He loves him and believes in him, but is outraged at the thought that there is ultimate truth; it offends his sense of justice. Isn't it interesting that when we speak to people who are not believers in Christ, everything hinges on the person of Jesus? People accuse Christians of being narrow-minded and it is a disaster when they are right, in this respect, but sometimes the confusion lies in confusing the words 'narrow' in definition, and 'narrow-minded'. The very reason Jesus was crucified revolves around the fact that he did not simply say he was 'a way' to the Father but 'the way, the truth and the life'. The road to which he pointed was narrow, but never narrow-minded. If you are exploring the Christian faith right, now, please understand the words of

Jesus – I am sure they were spoken with tears in his eyes, for no one agonized more than he did about those going to Christless eternity. Yet no one clearly believed in that possibility more than Jesus did; it cost him his life.

Peter says if we do not get built into the structure that has Jesus as its base, we will stumble over him and be offended by his claims, becoming like a Romanian house I heard of that was discovered to have been built onto the hillside without foundations… it will not take much for the entire building to slide into the valley and collapse! If we do not believe this, we will spend our life on fool's gold because we will not clearly see or believe in our hearts that the priorities lie elsewhere.

In Genesis 12, God declared to Abraham his original intention for the people of God. Adam had fallen, and God moved to Plan B: the creation of a nation, the Hebrew nation, that would bless every nation in the world. The problem was that the people of God then spent so much time and energy on becoming a viable nation that they forgot the second part of the promise and the contract: to bless every nation in the world. That is why Peter emphasizes to the new Israel, the church of Christ, this phrase 'you are…that you *may be*' (italics mine).

In Matthew 21, before he talks about being the cornerstone, Jesus tells the parable of a landowner who planted a vineyard and rented it out to vine dressers. At harvest time he sent slaves to collect the produce but the vine dressers beat, stoned or killed them. Finally he sent his son and heir, but the vine dressers killed him also so that the fruit of their labour could belong to them. The landowner returns in judgment to those who had acted with such injustice. Jesus turns to the Jewish religious leaders of the day and says, in effect: 'You have not stewarded the gift of this nation and all its physical and spiritual wealth in order to bless the world, so I need to find another race of people who will go out and change the world instead of you.' 'And you,' continues Peter, 'are that new nation!' Let us not miss the immense wealth at our disposal as the Jews did in Jesus' time, nor fail to bless the nations with it.

There are four distinguishing characteristics of this new people, the bride as she will be.

First we are a chosen race. The word for 'chosen' used by Peter is the same Greek word which he uses for Jesus being choice and precious. Jesus is chosen by God and precious – so are we. Jesus is the light of the world – so are we. Jesus is the foundation of the building – we are the bit people see. After our first joy at conversion we so often slump into seeing our faith as a struggle with sin until we finally make it to glory, but scripture says it is glorious, constantly evolving new birth!

I heard someone speaking about the way in which the film 'Snow White' had captured her imagination as a child. She would go outside and imagine herself as Snow White, with all the woodland creatures attending on her every desire, and a handsome prince coming to choose her above everyone else in the world. However, older sisters are sent to dampen such pretensions, and hers was no exception! Her sister told her that she couldn't marry a prince because you have to have royal blood to marry a prince, and her dreams were shattered! Later in life, the truth of scripture broke in upon her… her prince did come, and in saving her he gave her royal blood, and he is coming one day for us, his bride, upon a white horse, with 'King of kings' and 'Lord of lords' written upon his thigh.

If you are outside looking in upon Christianity it may seem that we are running an exclusive club with exclusive beliefs, but nothing should be further from the truth. We are ransomed royalty who, because we have new life, the Spirit of Jesus pulsating within us, are now members of the same race as him! Hallelujah!

As if that were not enough, Peter goes on to say that we are a royal priesthood. Ancient Jewish writings say that when the Messiah came he would be a king and a priest. He would wear a crown but it would be shaped like a mitre, and he would wear a priest's ephod, but it would be purple in colour. The extraordinary truth, says Peter, is that Jesus the Messiah has given us the amazing privilege of access to God, which only the high priest once had, because like him we are also now priests, a priesthood of all believers. We are to rule, restored to reign over sin, over circumstances, and over all that has been corrupted by the enemy since the dawn of time.

A priest's duties can be seen as a twofold ministry, an intercession that works both ways. Firstly, a priest is to bring people before God in prayer, pleading for forgiveness and mercy in every circumstance. In his book *Learning the Joy of Prayer*, Larry Lea encourages us to bring before God first ourselves, then our family and those whom we love, then our church, our nation and our world:

> 'God reigns over us when we obey Him, accept His rule and authority in our lives and become active in Jesus' kingdom movement to defeat evil, redeem sinners and bring mankind the blessings of God's reign. This, essentially, is what we are earnestly desiring when we declare

"Your Kingdom come. Your will be done". We are submitting to God and calling upon Him to perform His will on earth.

Consider the verbs in these two statements: Your kingdom come. Your will be done in earth as it is in heaven. In the Greek, the verbs are placed at the beginning of these two statements for emphasis. I cannot translate the meaning in any better way than to say that it is like a man firmly, decisively putting his foot down. "Come, kingdom of God! Be done, will of God!"[172]

Since reading Larry Lea's book, this concept has made a great deal of difference to the way I have prayed! Instead of a somewhat anxious bleating about the problems that I or others are facing, I have come before a mighty saviour and cried out, 'Come, kingdom of God in this situation! Establish your rule, Lord Jesus, how dare the enemy triumph over this? Be done, will of God in and for this person or this nation!' I continue to be specific concerning the things I am asking for, but faith rises inside me when I align myself with the will of God. I immediately see the inappropriateness of the enemy's whisper that it is all hopeless, and I begin to take my place then as a priest before God.

A priest does not just bring the people *before* God but he speaks to people *about* God. True gold is found in pleading before God for those we love, and crying out for his kingdom to come and his will to be done. But the second source of gold (and even more costly to us!) comes when we plead with people for God. As new believers we often joyfully espouse this calling without a second thought, and happily tell everyone who will listen to us about God's amazing kindness to us. However, as buckets of cold water are poured over us, and 'things' once again take up our hours, this calling becomes more and more difficult to fulfil. My only encouragement is that the more I push through to God's presence in prayer, the more the desires of his heart and the pleading of his Spirit will make a home in me again, and I will become desperate once more to plead with lost children.

Peter tells us next that we are a holy nation. Remember that in Matthew 21 Jesus told the religious leaders that the time had come for the Lord to move on to another nation, one that would not forget the punchline of blessing – a nation which would in turn bless all the nations of the earth. When Jesus speaks to the disciples of his second coming, he says, 'This gospel of the kingdom shall be preached in the whole world as a testimony to all the nations, and then the end will come.'[173] Jesus is deliberately returning to the promise made to Abraham: until every nation is blessed by the people of God, he will not go on to fulfil the promises. God is very single-minded about his plans. When Adam fouls up, he has a plan B in the nation of faith founded by Abraham. When that nation again falls through choosing fool's gold, he moves on to the church. So much time and effort today is spent on being what is seen to be a successful church, yet Jesus' anxiety is not that we are a successful church but that we are in the centre of the will of God!

The holy nation that Peter is referring to here is not one with an earthly capital or army – the Crusades show us bitterly what a disaster it is when the people of God shed blood to promulgate their faith. The often bloody history of the church has given the enemies of God potent ammunition to use against believers and we have much to repent of. Peter once again underlines that the only way that the people of God can change his world is as a *holy* nation. You or I may be the only evidence that our family, our friends, our work colleagues have that there is indeed a God of love and power! How do they observe this?

Peter says once more that it is our lifestyle, the simple fact that everything about our lives shows that we are only temporary residents in this world and our citizenship is elsewhere. Not that we spend the week in Christian meetings. Not that we go to the opposite extreme and are so much a part of the world that we blur the distinctions. We are to be people who are winsome with the presence of Jesus. We of all people know how to throw a good party, because we of all people should know how to celebrate. We of all people also resist the call of money but give it away with both hands and know how to live delightfully and creatively with less. As a holy nation our purpose is not to be within the walls of the church but outside! To be visible, different, winsome.

There is much anxious questioning in our day as to whether the church as such has died – whether we should cut our losses as the institutional church and go back to meeting in simple groups of believers, being salt and light where we are. Perhaps we are missing the point in some of these debates. How we 'package' the holy nation in the end does not really matter. Certainly we need to be far more relevant and creative in reaching our society and we will need to take church to others rather than expect them to show up at our doors. We will always need both building up with the word and the close presence of the

Lord building his throne as we worship together. But the point is not 'what should we throw out, what should we keep, how should we change?' so much as 'how can we reflect the power of God to our world?' The power of God is only found by first becoming a chosen race with Jesus, redeemed and set free to fly. It is to be found by taking our position as an intercessor between people and God and between God and people, pleading with broken hearts for salvation. It is to be found in a nation of people whose lifestyle is significantly different and attractive, who constantly and visibly affect the world about them for good. Our purpose is out there!

The church is often spoken of as 'a sleeping giant' One day as I pondered on this I realized that the thing about a recumbent posture is that no matter how huge the giant may be, it cannot be seen from a distance, or even beyond the nearest upright person. Much of our work as the people of God is horizontal...by which I mean it is directed towards man – evangelism, social action, care for the needy – all of which form the essential part of our calling as salt and light in the world. However, the problem with the giant when it stands up and becomes vertical is that it is immediately visible; attractive to some, threatening to others. Yet it is a force to be reckoned with from the perspective of both heaven and hell!

As I thought about these things, I read in the newspaper of the death of a thirteen-year-old girl. She had been consistently abused since the age of three, and at her death she had four sexually transmitted diseases in her body, had been forced into prostitution, and ended her miserable existence overdosing on drugs. As I read this story I saw yet again how desperate the need is for the giant to awaken! The people of God do have the potential of stretching into heaven and bringing the power of God down onto the earth they tread upon. If they rose as one, instead of majoring on their differences, how large would the giant be! And if they made their first priority the seeking of God's face, the giant would become vertical, God-aligned instead of man-aligned – then, and only then, society would see the difference. If we were once more vertical towards God we could also obtain a far broader perspective than we do when lying prostrate. I am reminded of the saying 'To fall is neither dangerous nor disgraceful; to remain prostrate may be both!' Upright, we might prove threatening, and we would certainly encounter far more opposition than we do at present, but our world would surely change. A holy nation would be on the march!

Finally we come to the beautiful phrase 'a people for God's own possession'.[174] Campbell Morgan, writing about this passage, says that the meaning of this phrase is similar to that when the Bible speaks of someone being demon-possessed.[175] By that phrase we understand that their mind, body, emotions and spirit are possessed, governed, by the evil one. This scripture says that we are to be a God-possessed people. Our thoughts, our words and our deeds are then determined by God himself. What a magnificent thought! Surely this is the deepest desire of every true lover of Christ: that he should so possess our every thought, word, emotion and action that people truly meet Jesus when they meet us. If this were our goal, everything else about our life would be subjected to this grand plan. We would plan our day so that our meeting with him could be significant, we would seek him and batter on the gates of heaven until he sent us his Spirit in power. We would be aware of the need to press in to him because we would become sensitive to our lack of his Spirit's fullness. We would plan with him the best way to meet his world's need both physically and spiritually. We would become a God-possessed people who heal the sick, and see his power in our neighbourhood, yes, but far more telling, our family would see us curb our temper, ask forgiveness when we fail, use our money generously, and demonstrate Jesus in the way we live our life before them. Certainly we will fail and fall, but if our passion is God-possession, everything around us will begin to change!

As I was praying one day I saw a vivid image of a church picnic. Everyone was seated on the grass, passing around food and chatting happily. Suddenly huge storm clouds rose on the skyline and someone said, 'It looks like rain', but the picnic carried on. The storm clouds began to move forwards and I saw field after field of standing grain beaten to the ground, but the people at the church picnic said, 'There's still time for a game of cricket!' There is simply no time left for fool's gold. God is calling us today to grow up and to take our amazing calling seriously. Not to be one thing at church and another at home, disillusioning the next generation. Not to gossip and backbite, to join petty factions or – worst of all – to do nothing at all. This is the time when we, the blood-bought bride of Christ are to move in our inheritance.

We all get tired of unrealistic, unachievable spiritual goals that leave us feeling second-rate. In fact sometimes we have constructed a mutual agreement with our fellow-believers to live normal lives with a bit of Christian truth tacked on so that we don't feel too compromised. Teaching

God-possession is terrifying! Yet actually if we look at every command Jesus ever made, they are impossible to fulfil without God-possession, so it must be achievable!

The problem of course is often to be found in our view of holiness. Sometimes we confuse the word 'holy' with 'holier-than-thou', and we shy away from such a concept, yet the most genuinely holy people I have been privileged to know are often the most human. They are quick to acknowledge their own failings, they are full of fun, interested in people and in everything that is going on, yet somehow there is also an 'otherness' about them. There is a depth of joy and peace that shines through them without their ever knowing it. If we need prayer, they are the one we want to go to because we know they walk closely with Jesus.

The thing is – let's be honest – we would like them to carry on and be that way, because it warms our hearts that there is someone, at least, who is like Jesus to whom we can go. We aspire to be like that, and some day when we have time to give to it, we will try to learn their secret, but for now it's enough that they are around! But try as we will, there is no mandate to be found in scripture for first- and second-class believers, and there is far too much need to leave a holy lifestyle to the few. It speaks volumes for the place our society has got to in the West that the hard work so often far outweighs the privilege when we learn what our inheritance really entails!

We have the life-blood of Jesus flowing through us, our spirit is literally cleansed by the blood he shed. We have the privilege of becoming priests for our family, for our friends, for our nation, for our world, and of moving angel armies by our heartbroken pleas! We can be a holy nation with its own language – I do not mean the kind of Christian psychobabble that completely excludes unbelievers. I mean that everything about us speaks hope that there is abundant life to be enjoyed. Perhaps most startling and wonderful of all, we can be a God-possessed people, those whose every word and action is controlled by the Spirit of the living God – quite literally Jesus-people whose lives are louder than their words.

11

Two Obituaries

These obituaries were written for people who chose the Kings' purse over fool's gold. They challenge us to go for gold, for that which is worth more than everything we strive for in this life.

I read the obituary column today.
Your *name was not there.*

There was a soldier.
Someone who had been brave in long-ago battles against a then-enemy. Mentioned in despatches. Decorated with ribbons for one final courageous exploit. Then many years in comparative wounded obscurity.

There was a politician.
A man who had impressed from his youth; had spiralled his way up the party and had held high office for many years, close to the royals, advising the monarch. Made a lord at the end of his days for serving the nation.

There was an athlete.
A woman who had excelled all who went before her. Records and gold medals filled her cabinet. Later years dedicated to charity work adding the laurel of kindness to her other trophies.

Finally there was a pop star.
A comparatively young man whose exploits on (and off) stage had
shocked and riveted his public. His fortune left between the latest
wife and a scattering of children around the world.

Your *name was not there.*

But there is another column in which your name is shining. Written
by the wounded hand of one known as the Lamb. It appears among
the names of those faithful to his call.

In this column, it tells of your strength; of the battles over our
forever-enemy. How you triumphed over sinful flesh. How you
held fast to the stronghold of truth in a day when your generation
surrendered the ground. How you prayed constantly over the
continents of the world. This was not a one-off battle but a
lifetime of valour in a cosmic war.

It tells of your faith. The simple wisdom of following your all-
powerful and all-wise king; the servant watching her sovereign's
hand, his eye — ready to do his bidding. Commended by him now
with the honour of 'good and faithful servant'.

It tells of your faithfulness, your daily training to be his athlete,
the discipline of a dedicated life; your hospitality and warmth;
your encouragement and comfort. No individual laurels for you, but
pleasure in being part of the great team.

It tells of your purity. A life of holiness, unremarkable on earth
but noted in heaven as a rare and precious gem fit for your heavenly
bridegroom, the value of your estate too great to be measured in
money, the bequest of lives brushing the reality of what is unseen

touched by your love

inspired by your faith

and left the legacy of your hope.

This was your life and we are so grateful for it.

....

'Well done, great relay runner, you have run your leg of
the race so well.
You have faithfully carried the baton from those faithful
men who passed it to you.
You have run that great race with such energy,
        such determination, such single-mindedness,
        such dedication, such inspiration, such zeal
        such grasp of the goal ahead.
You lived for the race; you loved it – it was your life.
Great is the crowd that applauds your arriving.
Greater by thousands because of the inspiration you
have been.
And now you have passed the winning post.
The laurel wreaths that you have are not for a grave, but
for a victor.
You have shown us how to run – wanting all for him and
nothing for yourself.

Simplicity was always your style, and how quickly the
tape finally came!
One minute still running strong, still loving the fellowship

of running together,
and then you were home; a few quick sighs and
you were there.
No regrets, no looking back – the Saviour's arms at last!
By now the brightness and the youth of heaven will be
yours.
So much to explore and see – but later.
Now the blessed joy of complete union with him.
The rest of being at his feet, of seeing him perfectly,
of understanding clearly, of hearing him
effortlessly.
Rest and a crown.
No more for you the rigours of training,
battle against sinful flesh, frustration of weak body.
Instead, perfect fulfilment.

The officials have come and gone from the track.
They were here for a few minutes, efficient, quick,
routine.
They know their job. They have cleared away and are
gone.

Now it is left to us.
Time has not stopped. There will be further days and
because of that, the race continues.
We have the baton now.
It was so reassuring to have you running that small
overlap of the way with us.
Now we are on our own.
We have to make the running,
to carry the baton faithfully,
so that others beyond us may pass it on.

Suddenly so much depends on how much we learned
from you − that is responsibility.
We are conscious of our inability,
      of our lack of so much that made you great.
If we run anything like as well as you, we shall be
      pleased.
Were it left to us we would have no hope
But we know that the master has given us the same Spirit
      which he had,
        and which you had,
And so we have hope.

May we run the race as faithfully as you did.

*These obituaries were written by my husband Nick for my father
and mother, Jack and Meg Stern, people who rejected all that
glitters and ran for the gold.*

Endnotes

1   Philippians 4:19

2   Job 23:10

3   Esther 4:16

4   This story is retold with the permission of General Sir Richard Dannatt.

5   Matthew 13:22

6   Eugene Peterson, *Reversed Thunder*, Harper Collins, 1988, p. xi.

7   Ross Paterson, *The Antioch Factor,* Sovereign World Ltd., 2000.

8   Mark Buchanan, *Your God is Too Safe*, Multnomah Publishers Inc., 2001.

9   Jim Cymbala, *Fresh Power*, Zondervan, 2001, p.121.

10   Philippians 3:8

11   Mark Buchanan, *Your God is Too Safe*, Multnomah Publishers Inc., 2001.

12   Matthew 8:5–10

13   Matthew 7:29

14   Job 23:8–10

15   Luke 4:1

16   Luke 4:14

17   Ephesians 6:13

18   Hebrews 4:15

19   1 Corinthians 3:12–15

20   Romans 5:3–4 (KJV)

21   Isaiah 58:8

22   G. Campbell Morgan, *Great Chapters of the Bible*, Marshall, Morgan and Scott, 1946.

23   Hannah Hurnard, *Hind's Feet on High Places*, CLC, 1955.

24 Romans 8:22–23

25 Eugene Peterson, *A Long Obedience in the Same Direction*,
    IVP, 1980.

26 Brother Lawrence, *The Practice of the Presence of God*,
    Baker Book House Co., 2007.

27 Luke 24:49

28 Genesis 1:2

29 Haggai 2:23

30 F. Brook, 'My Goal is God'

31 Source unknown

32   C.S. Lewis, *The Last Battle*, Collins, 2001.

33 1 Timothy 3:16

34 Stephen Hill, *Time To Weep*, Creation House, 1997.

35 Luke 24:53

36 F.J. Crosby, 'All The Way'.

37 Isaiah 66:9

38 Genesis 41:52

39 Eugene Peterson, *A Long Obedience in the Same Direction*, IVP, 1980.

40 Richard Foster, *Prayer*, Hodder & Stoughton, 1992,
    p.101.

41 See Psalm 139:7

42   John 14:9

43 Deuteronomy 1:31

44 Jim Cymbala, *Fresh Power*, Zondervan, 2001, p.125.

45 J.H. Jowett, *The Passion for Souls*, New York: Fleming
    H. Revell Co., 1905.

46 Hebrews 12:22–24

47 Charles Finney, *Lectures on Revival*, Bethany House
    Publishers, 1988, p.21.

48 Hebrews 12:29

49 David Wilkerson, *The Cross and the Switchblade*,
    Lakeland, 1979, p.7.

50   G.K. Chesterton, *Orthodoxy*, John Lane, 1909.

51   J.H. Jowett, *The Passion for Souls*, New York: Fleming
      H. Revell Co., 1905.

52   John Donne, 'Sermon No. 80', preached at the funeral of
      William Cockayne, 12 December 1626.

53   Psalm 100:4

54   Jeremiah 9:24

55   John 8:12

56   Matthew 5:14

57   Hebrews 5:7

58   Hans Christian Andersen, *The Snow Queen*, Walker
      Books, 2007.

59   Mark Rutland, *Streams of Mercy*, Vine Books, 1999.

60   Names have been changed.

61   Isaiah 58:8

62   2 Corinthians 10:3–5

63   Not her real name.

64   Deuteronomy 30:19

65   From the hymn 'O Worship the Lord' by J.S.B. Monsell.

66   Graham Kendrick, 'My True Feelings', Breaking of the
      Dawn, 1976.

67   From John Newton's hymn, 'Glorious Things of Thee are
      Spoken'.

68   John 4:28

69   Proverbs 13:12

70   John 7:38

71   Isaiah 58:12

72   Matthew 20:28

73   John 10:10

74   Matthew 18:11

75   Luke 12:49

76   C. Peter Wagner, *Territorial Spirits*, Sovereign World,
      1991, p.4.

77   George S Patton, quoted online in a review of his book

War as I Knew It, Mariner Books, 1995.

78 C.S. Lewis, *The Screwtape Letters*, HarperCollins, 1942.

79 1 John 3:8

80 Matthew 11:4–6

81 Adrian Plass, *Clearing Away the Rubbish*, Monarch, 1988.

82 C.S. Lewis, *The Lion, the Witch and the Wardrobe*, Collins, 2001.

83 1 Chronicles 16:22

84 Mark 11:25

85 Ephesians 6:10

86 Psalm 29:4–5

87 Ephesians 6:12

88 Ephesians 6:12

89 Graham Kendrick, 'All Heaven Waits'.

90 Matthew 16:3

91 2 Peter 3:12

92 Hosea 8:7

93 2 Thessalonians 2:8–10

94 Matthew 24:37 (NIV)

95 Acts 5:41

96 Arthur Hugh Clough, 'Say Not The Struggle'.

97 John 4:21–24

98 Not her real name.

99 Merlin Carothers, *Prison To Praise*, Hodder & Stoughton, 1996.

100 1 Thessalonians 5:16–18

101 Ephesians 5:20

102 C.S. Lewis, *Reflections on the Psalms*, HarperCollins, 1974, pp.79–80.

103 1 Timothy 1:11

104 Psalm 100:4

105 Catherine Marshall, *Something More*, Hodder &

Stoughton, 1974

106 2 Chronicles 20:15–17

107 Habakkuk 3:17–19

108 Isaiah 53:3

109 Psalm 45:7

110 2 Chronicles 20:22

111 Source unknown

112 2 Samuel 23:1

113 Psalm 13:4–6

114 1 Thessalonians 5:16–18

115 Acts 2:47

116 John 3:30

117 Romans 12:1–2

118 Psalm 22:3

119 Source unknown

120 Taken from *My Utmost for His Highest* by Oswald
     Chambers, ©1935 by Dodd Mead & Co., renewed ©1963
     by the Oswald Chambers Publications Assn., Ltd. Used by
     permission of Discovery House Publishers, Grand Rapids
     MI 49501. All rights reserved.

121 John 4:23–24

122 2 Samuel 6:20–23

123 Mark 12:41–44

124 Psalm 24:3–4

125 Tommy Tenney, 'God's Favourite House', Destiny Image
     Publishers Inc., 1999

126 Exodus 33:16

127 2 Samuel 6:1–12

128 Psalm 84:10

129 John S.B. Monsell, 'O Worship the Lord', *Hymns of Love
     and Praise*, London: Bell and Daldy, 1863.

130 George Herbert, 'Love', *The Complete English Poems*,
     Penguin, 1992

131 Isaiah 58:6–12

133 Psalm 119:32

134 Luke 10:25–27

135 Chuck Colson, *Loving God*, Hodder & Stoughton, 1987.

136 Isaiah 58:7.

137 C.S. Lewis, *The Lion, the Witch and the Wardrobe*, Harper Collins, 1950.

138 Ezekiel 22:30

139 Isaiah 58:12

140 Adrian Plass, *Clearing Away The Rubbish*, Monarch, 1988.

141 Luke 9:23

142 www.raymayhewonline.com

143 James Boswell, *The Life of Samuel Johnson*, Signet Classics, 1968.

144 Revelation 12:10

145 Hebrews 5:8

146 Ephesians 2:14

147 Genesis 50:20

148 Romans 7:18

149 Joel 2:25

150 Speaking at Spring Harvest seminar, 1996.

151 1 Corinthians 2:2

152 Matthew 5:45

153 2 Corinthians 4:4

154 Tom Utley, 'Simple English for the Church of England', *Daily Telegraph*, 7 January 2005. (Taken from http://www.telegraph.co.uk/opinion/main.jhtml?xml=/opinion/2005/01/07/do0702.xml.)

155 2 Chronicles 32:31

156 Ronald Dunn, *When Heaven is Silent*, CLC Publications, 2008.

157 Genesis 50:20

158 Isaiah 53:3

159 Psalm 45:7

160 Margery Williams, *The Velveteen Rabbit*, Camelot, 1975.

161 Gerald Coates, *Kingdom Now!*, Kingsway, 1993, pp.105–108.

162 John 15:15 (ASV)

163 1 Corinthians 1:18

164 Acts 2:13

165 2 Corinthians 12:9

166 Acts 2:44–46

167 Genesis 2:25

168 C.S. Lewis, *The Great Divorce*, Fount, 2002.

169 Ray Mayhew, 'In My Father's House', found at http://www.raymayhewonline.com/igsbase/igstemplate.cfm?SRC=DB&SRCN=&GnavID=10&SnavID=40.

170 1 Peter 2:4–12

171 C.S. Lewis, *The Voyage of the Dawn Treader*, Penguin, 1952.

172 Larry Lea, *Learning the Joy of Prayer*, Creation House, 1987.

173 Matthew 24:14

174 1 Peter 2:9

175 G. Campbell Morgan, *Peter and the Church*, Pickering and Inglis, 1937, p.77.

TREASURES OF DARKNESS

Grace Turner is Director of Firelighters which is a training and mission agency. Early in 2008 they launched a new Charity called Treasures of Darkness based on Isaiah 45v3 "I will give you the treasures of darkness and hidden wealth of secret places, in order that you may know that it is I, the Lord, the God of Israel, who calls you by your name".

The strap line of Treasures of Darkness is "Sell your chains to break theirs" and the challenge given is to donate a piece of valuable jewellery or other "treasure" that can be sold and the proceeds used to rescue children who are sold into slavery. Treasures of Darkness partners with two projects – one in W.Africa which is involved in rescuing children at risk of slavery in the cocoa plantations, and the other project rescues little girls sold into prostitution in Cambodia.

Look them up on www.treasuresofdarkness.org.uk